Living

with

Fibromyalgia

Living

with

Fibromyalgia

4 Steps to Manage Pain and Lead a Fulfilling Life

DEAN L. MONDELL, M.D., AND PATTI WRIGHT

McGraw·Hill

New York   Chicago   San Francisco   Lisbon   London   Madrid   Mexico City
Milan   New Delhi   San Juan   Seoul   Singapore   Sydney   Toronto

Library of Congress Cataloging-in-Publication Data

Mondell, Dean L.
    Living with fibromyalgia : 4 steps to manage pain and lead a fulfilling life /
    Dean L. Mondell and Patti Wright.— 1st ed.
        p.   cm.
    Includes bibliographic references and index.
    ISBN 0-07-145148-X (alk. paper)
    1. Fibromyalgia—Popular works.   I. Wright, Patti.   II. Title.
    RC927.3.M66   2005
    616.7'42—dc22   2005003887

2 3 4 5 6 7 8 9 0   DOC/DOC   0 9 8 7 6 5

ISBN 0-07-145148-X

Consult with your physician or counselor before taking any medications or performing any exercises discussed in this book. This book is not a replacement for medical advice. Characters and examples herein are fictitious and any resemblance to any persons living or dead is coincidence. The stories taken from interviews are true, but the names and other identifying characteristics have been changed to protect their privacy.

*To my mom, Gladys Kerekes, who suffered from
fibromyalgia until passing in 1993*

—Patti Wright

CONTENTS

◉

FOREWORD

By Lynne Matallana, President, National Fibromyalgia Association*

◉

I HAVE HEARD the desperation in your voice and seen the apprehension and trepidation on your face. I know how alone, afraid, and unprepared you feel about what lies ahead of you. Yet I also know that for those of us with fibromyalgia there is hope for a better tomorrow.

Today, you, like millions of people in our country, must face the challenges of living with the symptoms and consequences of fibromyalgia. Its complexity and unpredictability can challenge the core of your internal strength. Its chronic nature can turn your world upside down and change your life forever. But just like everything in your life, you can take back control and prepare yourself for the challenges that you will face. With reliable information and a well-organized plan of options, you can embrace your new life so as to restore and maintain a fulfilling future.

Living with Fibromyalgia: 4 Steps to Manage Pain and Lead a Fulfilling Life is a complete guide to help you to better understand your illness and it suggests steps that you can take to help rebuild your life. It exposes the myths of fibromyalgia and helps you explore your options so that you can maximize the benefits of your self-management efforts. This book's step-by-step process is designed to inspire, encourage, and assist you in discovering how to manage your fibromyalgia. You won't want to just read this book; you will want to live it!

PREFACE

By Daniel T. Shiode, Ph.D., Clinical Psychologist

◉

FIBROMYALGIA (FM) IS A disease that creates havoc in a person's life as it affects the lives of those around him or her. Like any life-changing illness, FM affects a person's physical, mental, and spiritual well-being. As a clinical psychologist practicing in the field of pain psychology, I am often faced with the daunting task of helping people afflicted with FM successfully adapt to life with this life-disrupting illness. This is a difficult task under the best of circumstances.

Like anyone with a chronic illness, every person with FM wants the pain and sickness to go away, and they long to have their old healthy lives back. My clients struggle with the realization that their lives won't be the same as they were before FM—that the losses/changes are permanent. Yet, for these persons, life itself is not at stake. The future waits, and the formidable task of building a fulfilling future becomes the primary agenda.

The task—we should say multiple tasks that are formidable in appearance—is to identify and utilize the capacities and resources that remain. Too often we focus only on the losses without acknowledging the strengths that may be unaffected. A full accounting of these strengths often shows that they are considerable. In this way we can devise a rewarding future.

Designing the future is our necessary task, since the present way of living brings little or no satisfaction. FM can leave a person unable to carry on as before, frozen in a dilemma of inaction. The chronic illness persists and life goes on in motionless misery. Depression and despair can follow in its wake. Acceptance of loss by itself does not bring resolution to the dilemma of inaction. Fortunately, a remarkable feature of human nature is to adapt, to assess circumstances, and to use our innate resourcefulness to devise new means of coping.

The Four-Step Plan described in *Living with Fibromyalgia* brings structure to these tasks by providing a simple, yet elegant outline that can help to guide both counselor/psychotherapist and patient through the difficult and complicated process of adapting to a life-changing illness. It does so in a way that is pragmatic for clients and conceptually sound for clinicians. The strategy in the Four-Step Plan is innovative in its organization yet consonant with the principles of adapting to chronic illness. Psychotherapy, or counseling, integrating this approach can provide patients with FM the opportunity to successfully come to terms with and adapt to the life changes caused by their illness, at a pace that is right for them.

The basis of the Four-Step Plan to Adaptation is that of taking an active, adaptive training approach that helps people live more effectively with FM. It encourages people with FM to complete a practical sequence of tasks to accommodate their lifestyle to the realities of FM. In Step One, you get your bearings and resolve your reactions and losses. You get blocks out of your way and redirect your attention toward a more positive determination regarding the future. In Step Two, you take the initiative and gather your tools, recruiting complete care and setting up family roles. In Step Three, you are ready to begin rebuilding your life to accommodate FM. In Step Four, you protect what you have built. Fibromyalgia is notorious for destabilizing lives and knocking down what you have built. Safeguards are developed to protect your accomplishments.

Any person or family with FM who reads *Living with Fibromyalgia* cannot help but feel that the discussions resonate with their particular condition; yet these principles can apply to people suffering from any chronic illness or condition. It is my hope that future editions of these strategies will specifically focus on some of these other conditions.

Hopefully, then, this book will be the first in a series on adapting to chronic illness. The clustering of tasks into workable parcels and sequencing of tasks into stepwise progressions provide a fresh and workable approach to adaptation. It is a highly versatile and practical approach, structuring the adaptation process in a manner understandable for laypersons and conceptually useful for professionals.

ACKNOWLEDGMENTS

◉

WE WISH TO THANK our editors Natasha Graf and Jenn Tust for their vision in supporting this message of hope and their hard work in presenting it to you. Heartfelt thanks go to our agent, Marilyn Allen, for the blessing of her friendship and incredible support in making this lifelong work a reality. Special thanks to our publisher, McGraw-Hill, for recognizing the need to help fibromyalgia patients and their loved ones adapt to this chronic illness and for giving us the opportunity to bring this new concept to the public.

The authors would also like to thank many professionals and support-group advisors who have contributed their expertise to this ten-year project, including Daniel T. Shiode, Ph.D.; Allan Chino, Ph.D.; Corinne Davis, M.D.; David Guyette, M.S.; Mervyn D. Willard, M.D.; Ray and Tracy Brach and Scott Davis, Esq.

Our greatest teachers have been the thousands of patients, loved ones, and members of the Fibromyalgia Friends Support Group of Nevada who participated in our polls and interviews and who shared their stories. We are grateful to them for their invaluable assistance in adding truth and reality to our research and conclusions.

Special thanks to Christy Noble for being the rock of FMFSG and whose ongoing service made all of this work possible. We greatly appreciate Lynne Matallana, of the National Fibromyalgia Association, for her many years of support and encouragement. Sincere appreciation for the contributions of Mattie Mitchell-Smith, M.S., who has believed in this work and inspired us every step of the way.

We are deeply grateful to Vicki and Frank Fertitti and the wonderful people at all of the Station Casinos; their moral and financial support of our nonprofit work kept the "sharing and caring" research alive. Without their help, we would not be where we are today.

We thank God for blessing us with this lifelong work, for bringing us together with you, and for the opportunity to continue reaching out to help you realize your dearest wishes—a fulfilling and productive life.

INTRODUCTION

◉

FIBROMYALGIA (FM) is disruptive to the lives of everyone it touches, yet few techniques and little information are widely available to help stabilize and protect people with FM. For *Living with Fibromyalgia*, we consulted references on chronic illness, gathered input from patient surveys and interviews, and compiled various materials from our years of working with FM-affected families. The Four Steps to Adaptation, which are the focus of this book, evolved from this work. You are holding a comprehensive guide for easing symptoms, informing loved ones, and helping sufferers learn how to rebuild and manage fulfilling lifestyles despite FM.

FM is not curable, but it is treatable. It will be your companion forever. You have a choice: let the illness manage you or take control of your own life. You don't have to allow a chronic illness to destroy everything you hold dear—family, home, work, friendships. When your health condition changes, it affects everyone you know and everything you do; it is a mistake to think you can be okay without making adjustments to the new reality of FM. Our Four-Step Plan shows you how to ease the struggle with your changing situation a step at a time.

ABOUT THIS BOOK

Fibromyalgia changes everything, but it doesn't have to ruin your life. If you are in constant battle with FM, your symptoms will control you. Chapters 1 and 2 discuss the medical aspects of FM to help ease your symptoms.

HOW THE FOUR STEPS EVOLVED

The Four Steps to Adaptation concept evolved out of the urgent need for people to learn how to live well with FM. It discusses how to deal with the social and emotional challenges after being diagnosed with FM; and these are the issues that will make or break you. Your life success depends on your ability to cope and learn to construct and maintain a new lifestyle.

I (Patti Wright), have had FM all of my life and know that every person touched by this disease needs help. While I grew into adulthood with fibromyalgia there was little research and reliable information available. It was not until the mid-1990s that resources began to emerge. This was around the time that a few friends with FM and I started getting together to share information and offer each other support. Word got around, and today ours is a support group of over 1,500 people. The more we learned, the more we needed to understand this disease, and with the help of many friends and medical and psychological experts, pieces of the FM puzzle kept falling into place.

As we watched the information grow, we discovered that it didn't explore how to cope and live a satisfying life with FM. This was a crucial area that needed to be addressed. Both FM patients and everyone connected to them needs help in this area. This problem required specific answers—a plan that people could follow to get on with their lives and be okay.

To answer the questions of fibromyalgia, we needed a special combination of information, life experience, and analysis to create a cohesive plan of action. Finally, our workable system of adapting came together.

What It Means to Adapt to Fibromyalgia

To adapt means to make a series of life adjustments to achieve quality of living. To cope successfully requires that you complete many tasks. The adaptation process can be compared to the mourning process in some ways. To recover from the loss of someone dear to you, you need to progress through a series of emotional tasks. Getting through the mourning process leads to your emotional recovery and the ability to deal with loss of a loved one. FM affects your order of living in much the same way. By adjusting to losses and changes, you and your loved ones can regain a sense that life is worthwhile and find stability again.

ORIENTATION TO THE FOUR STEPS TO ADAPTATION

Without really understanding the tasks of adapting, the work may seem overwhelming. The Four Steps cluster the tasks into manageable stages. Each step offers a group of tasks that allows you to tackle the job in a simple way: one task at a time.

In this book, a step is a series of related tasks and skills needed to rebuild a satisfying life. Each step is a challenge, and success at one step is the entryway to the next. By focusing your efforts on the Four Steps one at a time, you make decisive and steady progress toward a higher quality of living. Within every step are tasks for both you and your loved ones. The tasks of loved ones are not identical to yours, and the speed of each person's progress may be different. But make no mistake— for forward progress to occur, your entire family needs to be involved in this work.

Step One: Assess Your Reactions to Fibromyalgia

How do you feel about this new reality? You take the first step by appraising your present emotional responses to FM. The journey continues as you resolve these reactions. In Chapter 3, we describe the most common reactions to FM and how to resolve them.

Remember that each person enters the process with a different mind-set, so the tasks in Step One are not exactly the same for everyone. You may be entering the adapting process with a (preexisting) block or barrier in place, and you need to resolve these blocks before you can move forward. Managing these barriers is different from dealing with reactions to FM, so refer to Chapter 7 for more information.

Step Two: Take Responsibility for Finding Care and Learning to Adapt

The transition to Step Two is an exciting but difficult task. You come to terms with what you are up against in order to manage your life with FM. Step Two requires you to take responsibility and initiative to take back control of your life. You actively seek out the right care. We were surprised to find from our support group that many FM people are hesitant about finding and receiving proper care. Work at Step Two helps you overcome this hesitation because you see that FM is mainly your responsibility alone—no one else is going to do it—so you must do everything possible to readjust your way of thinking to start finding a lifestyle that works best for you.

Step Three: Rebuild Your Life and Your Relationships

Step Three discusses rebuilding your life in six areas: self-worth, time and energy, family life, relationships with loved ones, social life, and job or career. Focusing on these areas will help you make the lifestyle changes you need to live the fullest life possible with FM. You will feel a sense of peace settling over you as your fight with the world settles down and your life starts to feel comfortable. This means less stress and certainly an easing of your pain and other symptoms. Can you do it? Of course! Most people quickly rediscover strengths, talents, and skills that allow them to design a new and rewarding future.

Step Four: Stabilize Fibromyalgia by Managing Stress and Crises

Your new lifestyle is a great achievement—something you need to protect. Having made it this far, you want to maintain it. You may be vulnerable at first, so be careful and safeguard all that you have built. Step Four covers stress management in detail since stress is the primary cause of major setbacks. You'll learn to cultivate better living skills and continue to grow.

GUIDES FOR YOUR JOURNEY THROUGH THE FOUR STEPS

We will serve as your guides each step of the way. It will take time and effort to learn all the new skills and techniques to rebuild your relationships, stabilize stress, and adjust to a new life pattern. It is very hard work; and it does not happen overnight. Throughout the process of adaptation, you are developing new ways of viewing and doing things. With each step comes confidence in knowing that the lessons are becoming part of the new way you think and react. Everything you learn helps you build the strength to go a little bit further—until your goals begin to become realty. By Step Four, you will have management skills in all areas of your life to both protect your new lifestyle and to continue your journey. The beauty of adaptation is that the pattern you develop will be with you throughout your life and it will grow and change with you.

Take a deep breath, remind yourself to be patient, and turn the page.

Living

with

Fibromyalgia

RECOGNIZING KEY SYMPTOMS

◉

Fibromyalgia (FM) is a syndrome, a constellation of symptoms about which patients complain but little is often identified upon medical examination. It is a problem of pain and dysfunction experienced by millions of people in the United States and worldwide. Although it affects a higher percentage of women, it also strikes men and children of all ages. The name Fibromyalgia Syndrome (FMS) is also used for this disorder, as the term *syndrome* denotes a combination of symptoms and signs that are often found together. Symptoms of fibromyalgia may fluctuate in severity and may improve with treatment, but cures and total remissions are rarely seen.

Looking at FM from the inside out, what you see is not what you get. Books about illnesses usually begin with a description of the disorder's symptoms or ways to identify or define the disease being discussed. These books start with a medical definition, and then discuss the symptoms one by one. It is extremely difficult, however, to explain a lifelong chronic illness such as FM—when the story is just so outrageous as to seem unbelievable. Nevertheless, we will start here by explaining the common symptoms of FM and begin the story about one small part of it.

IDENTIFYING COMMON SYMPTOMS OF FIBROMYALGIA

Fibromyalgia can be very confusing because its symptoms may give you only one clue about what is going on. Often, the first sign is feeling tired and aching all over—like you have the flu and it just won't go away. Or the symptoms may begin with chronic headaches or with any of several other symptoms.

The criteria used by the American College of Rheumatology (ACR) for a diagnosis of fibromyalgia includes: widespread pain present for at least three months; pain on both sides of the body; pain above and below the waist; axial skeletal pain; and pain in 11 of the 18 tender points. Other symptoms described by patients with fibromyalgia include fatigue, non-restorative sleep, morning stiffness, frequent headaches and neck aches, irritable bowel syndrome, slowed cognition or mental processing, decreased endurance, and poor coordination.

When the ACR first published its list of symptoms in 1990, the world began to look more seriously at this illness. Fibromyalgia finally had a name and a description.

Widespread Pain

Unexplained pain everywhere that comes and goes is a sign that something is wrong, and it is often the reason people start looking for answers. Such severe pain can be frightening for you and those around you. People who have never experienced severe pain may find it difficult to understand how disabling and worrisome it can be when there are no visible reasons for what is happening.

Fibromyalgia patients describe their pain in many ways. Some of the most common adjectives include aching, stabbing, knife-like stiffness, everywhere, increased after exercise or activity, and associated with weakness. The term *widespread pain* in regard to FM refers to the entire body—not to one specific area. While the pain of FM is widespread, one region of the body may be more affected than other regions. For example, some patients can report symptoms of pain beginning in regions of their body under repetitive use, stress, or strain.

Pain also occurs at local sites called *tender points*—typically in areas where muscles attach to bone or ligament—and radiates out from them. (See Figure 1.1.) Many practitioners can perform tender point exams and make a definite diagnosis.

With FM, you may also feel pain in your joints. However, your joints do not become inflamed or deformed as they would be with such inflammatory conditions as rheumatoid arthritis.

Traditional medical treatment options for FM pain are covered in Chapter 2.

Muscle and Joint Stiffness

As an FM sufferer, you may feel stiffness in your muscles and joints. This stiffness is usually worse after you have slept or after you have sat in one position for a period

FIGURE 1.1 TENDER POINTS TYPICALLY FOUND IN FIBROMYALGIA

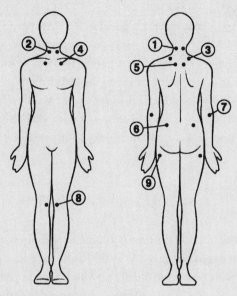

1. The insertion of the suboccipital muscles at the base of the skull
2. Anterior aspect of lower neck—intertranverse spaces between C5 and C7 vertebrae.
3. The trapezius muscle in the midpoint of the upper border
4. The costochondral junctions, of the second ribs
5. At the origins of the supraspinatus muscles above the scapular spine
6. The gluteus medius muscle, upper outer area of the buttock
7. 1 to 2 cm distal of the epicondyles of the elbow (tennis elbow)
8. The medial, upper knee, proximal to the joint line
9. The greater trochanter (top of the thighbone)

of time without stretching or moving. This stiffness after waking or staying in one position is sometimes termed morning stiffness, or gelling, and occurs frequently in computer operators or others who sit most of the time. You will probably be more comfortable during the day if you vary your activities and do not stay confined in one position for very long. Some FM patients experience swelling along with joint stiffness, which closely mimics rheumatoid arthritis, and this occasional unexplained swelling is not confined to joints.

THE DANGER OF COMPARING FIBROMYALGIA
TO OTHER RHEUMATIC DISEASES

Fibromyalgia is often compared to rheumatic diseases, but FM is not an inflammatory disease. When faced with such enormous pain and so many unpredictable symptoms, you may want to compare it to another disease in order to have a "set point" to work from. However, this type of comparative thinking brings up alarming thoughts because of only one common symptom. Remember that there is nothing you can compare FM with; it is a disease unique to itself. You cannot define it or explain it by likening it to another disorder. You will only know what it is if you have it or if you live with someone who does.

Fatigue

Besides pain, just feeling tired all the time is a common symptom. Profound fatigue is a good clue that something is amiss. As an FM sufferer, your fatigue may be so severe as to interfere with your regular daily activities, such as your job or physical activity at home. Exertion on one day often causes next-day feelings of illness, or postexertional malaise. Overexertion can be the downfall of just trying to live a normal life. Your fatigue may be worsened by severe pain and loss of sleep, but it usually improves as these symptoms are corrected.

Unrefreshed and Interrupted Sleep

With fibromyalgia, you may feel that you wake up feeling worse than when you went to sleep—even to the point of feeling as though you have not slept at all. Along with pain, disrupted sleep is usually one of the first symptoms that needs to be addressed. Controlling both sleep and pain can make a tremendous difference in your life.

Disturbed sleep has been linked in part to abnormal alpha-delta brain waves that are commonly observed during sleep in FM patients. The percentage of time spent in deep sleep, as opposed to shallow sleep, is often less in FM sufferers than in normal subjects.

There are a variety of medications for helping abnormal sleep and insomnia. You may even require more than one medication to help you achieve sound sleep. By trial and error, you and your physician can work out the medication regimen that permits you adequate sleep. Remember to also practice good sleep habits. Make sure to go to bed at about the same time each night. Make it a priority to do relaxing things prior to bedtime to be ready for sleep.

Nocturnal Leg Jerking/Restless Legs Syndrome

If your spouse complains that you sleep "like a moving windmill," then you probably have nocturnal myoclonus, or periodic limb movement disorder, which is another common FM symptom. You may not even realize that you have this symptom until someone asks you about it. Nocturnal leg movement is most prominent in the very early hours of the morning. The muscles in motion are not confined to your legs and may also include your arms, neck, and other muscle groups. In some cases, jerking may cause your whole body to move violently.

In the morning, you may find that the muscles involved in the jerking are sore. Another consequence of muscles jerking is that your normal sleep pattern is disrupted so that you are not able to reach the deep stage of sleep that is necessary to feel rested as frequently. In time, this disrupted sleep can take its toll on everyone in your family.

The medication usually prescribed to calm restless legs syndrome is Klonopin—the generic name is clonozepam—and many FM sufferers do very well on it. However, you may feel some drag-over tiredness or sleepiness into the next day when using this drug. It is potent and long acting, so make sure you are in a comfortable place before you take it. And when starting a new medication like this, remember to start cautiously and adjust the dosage carefully, using a pill-cutter if necessary.

Mood Symptoms

Which came first, fibromyalgia or depression? That's a good question. Depression, anxiety, and panic are common among FM patients. You may have experienced these symptoms even before the onset of FM. You may experience them as a response to the ordeal of being ill and find them to be exacerbated by pain, fatigue, and other life-disrupting symptoms. Or your mood symptoms may be part of the syndrome of FM, brought on with the onset of the rest of the FM symptoms. Researchers name two causes of anxiety and depression in people with FM: first, the ordeal of a chronic illness could cause anxiety and depression in anyone; and second, anxiety and depression are part of FM, beginning at the same time as the other symptoms of the illness.

Whatever the cause of the depression, medication can help and is one of many considerations to discuss with your doctor. Most FM patients can benefit from medications that boost the serotonin levels in the brain: Prozac, Effexor, Cymbalta, Paxil, Elavil, Zoloft, and Lexapro. These medications, especially in higher doses, may improve mood problems as well as other symptoms, including pain and lack of energy. An effective way to proceed with combating depression is to try several medications and test various doses before settling on the one that works best for you. Again, work closely with your doctor to find the right medications.

Fibro Fog, or Slowed Mental Processing

Another symptom you may experience is mental confusion, often referred to as *fibro fog*. In particular, you may find that concentration and focus are difficult or that you often feel "out of it." This is a frequent complaint as most FM patients tend to be very responsible and intelligent people. Thus, it is extremely stressful to recognize signs of forgetfulness or memory loss in yourself.

Fibro fog can be demonstrated and proven on timed cognitive tests. For example, on a reading comprehension test, you will do as well as those without FM— unless the time is restricted. Similarly, if you are doing mental tasks on a computer, you can perform them as well as those who do not have FM, but you may not be able to work as fast and complete the same quantity of work. While there is no prescribed treatment for fibro fog, there are some basic tips that the Arthritis Foundation recommends for you to put into practice to help ease you out of your mental confusion.

- Use repetition

- Write things down

- Get the proper amount of sleep

- Use your best time of day to accomplish the most work

- Take care of your medical needs

- Keep physically and mentally active

- Get help and support from loved ones

- Minimize noise and distractions

- Don't take on more than you can handle

Irritable Bowel Syndrome

Irritable bowel syndrome (IBS) is a colonic condition characterized by constipation, crampy diarrhea, or both in an alternating cycle. IBS is a problem for many FM patients, but you should be able to control it moderately well with a high-fiber diet and such medications as Bentyl and Zelnorm. Recent studies show that a combination of a high-fiber diet plus a medication of the selective serotonin reuptake inhibitor class, such as Prozac, also works well. Bouts of IBS can be irritating enough that you may have to stay home for a few days, but they usually pass. Your primary care physician can usually handle IBS, but if problems persist, he or she may refer you to a gastroenterologist.

Bladder Spasms and Urinary Frequency

Bladder spasms or urinary frequency, accompanied by bloating and an uncomfortable feeling of pressure, is also a symptom of fibromyalgia. If your symptoms of this nature persist and are accompanied by severe pain, you may need to seek help. Although rare in the general population, a painful bladder condition called *interstitial cystitis (IC)* occurs with moderate frequency in FM patients and requires a checkup with a urologist.

Gastrointestinal Problems

Chances are good that as an FM patient, you suffer from additional or overlapping illnesses, which means that you may take more than one medication. A common result of mixing medications is acid reflux or chronic heartburn, which along with sensitivity to acidic foods and many other causes, can damage your esophagus and gastrointestinal tract. If your reflux or heartburn problems are severe, you might want your doctor to refer you to a gastroenterologist.

Severe Headaches

Several types of headaches, including migraine, sinus, and muscle tension headaches, are another quite common symptom of fibromyalgia. Sinus headaches affect your sinus areas, eyes, or top of your head. Muscle tension headaches usually begin in the back of your neck and go around your entire head like a vise. Migraines typically affect one side of the head, usually pound or throb, and can be accompanied by blurred vision, nausea, or sensitivity to light or sound. Some people get tingling, pins-and-needles sensations in one arm or leg, and some describe a strange odor. These are multiple types of headaches common to FM, and you may have more than one type of headache or a combination of factors in play, so be prepared to state the location and precise nature of your headache when you see a doctor. Sinus headaches appear to be the most common type experienced, and they can often be treated with over-the-counter medicines. If your headaches are severe, you may want to ask your doctor to refer you to a neurologist.

Allergy-like Symptoms

Researchers are just beginning to acknowledge that allergy-like symptoms, such as sniffling and sneezing, can accompany FM. With your body in hypersensitive mode, you may experience allergies of all kinds, especially during seasonal changes that bring pollens and dust into the air. You may be one of the 10 to 35 percent of FM patients who report dry mouth or dry eyes, with the most frequent complaint being burning and stinging eyes. Your primary care physician can usually address this problem, especially if he or she is an allergy and asthma specialist.

Balance Problems and Dizziness

Fibromyalgia can create balance problems that, if severe, can give you a tendency to fall. The dangers of falling include bodily injury, especially head injury, and a flare-up of FM symptoms. Most physical therapy offices or rehabilitation centers offer treatment programs and exercises for balance and coordination difficulties. Your doctor can also prescribe specific medications for easing problems with vertigo and dizziness.

Tingling or Numbness in the Hands and Feet

With FM, you may experience tingling or numbness in your hands or feet. Many clinicians say that tingling and numbness are probably just anxiety, but FM patients are reporting these symptoms more frequently than not. Researchers are now acknowledging this association, probably because neuralgia, or painful nerve symptoms, is so common among FM people.

Painful Menstrual Symptoms

If you are female and of childbearing age, you may experience overall heightened pain and sensitivity during your menstrual cycles. Besides bloating, swelling, and lower back aches, bouts with IBS are also common. Menstrual migraines may also be a problem. However, nonsteroidal anti-inflammatory agents (compounds used to treat arthritis), and for some patients, antidepressants can be used to help PMS symptoms.

Unexplained Weight Gain or Loss

There is usually a reasonable explanation for weight fluctuations with FM. Mood swings that accompany the onset of a chronic illness can affect your eating habits and cause you to either gain or lose weight. Likewise, decreased physical activity or exercise can affect your weight. If you experience nausea, vomiting, or other unusual symptoms, tell your physician. If weight gain is a concern, be sure to mention this when you and your doctor begin discussing medications to control your FM symptoms.

Noncardiac Chest Pain

With FM, you may feel chest pain that mimics that of heart disease or a heart attack. Mitral valve prolapse (MVP) often occurs in conjunction with FM and is one possibility to consider. MVP sensations are caused by connective tissue that doesn't flex as it should, which could result in chest pains. Many other conditions can also create tightness or pain in your chest. Chest pain is a symptom worth noting, especially if you also suffer from diabetes, as researchers are now viewing diabetics as potential heart patients. Make sure to tell your doctor if you have persisting chest pain.

POSSIBLE CAUSES OF FIBROMYALGIA

No one knows what causes fibromyalgia, but there are a number of unproven theories under investigation. FM was once thought to be a soft-tissue disorder—soft-tissue rheumatism—but this hypothesis has been disproved and discarded. Other theories now link FM with chronic fatigue syndrome (CFS), irritable bowel syndrome, premenstrual syndrome, and Gulf War illness. To date, we know of no provoking insult that causes FM. Several predisposing conditions or triggering insults, however, have been associated with the onset of FM. Some of them are listed below, although further research is needed to confirm or disprove them.

Genetics

Fibromyalgia, like many other illnesses, seems to run in families. Many FM patients now recognize that a grandfather or, more often, a mother presented symptoms like their own but were never diagnosed with anything specific. Specific genes that cause FM have not yet been identified, although the same can be said for many illnesses. We expect these genes to be identified in the future.

Family patterns are very evident in support group situations because whole families will come for help together on a monthly basis. It is not unusual to see two or even three generations from one family sitting together at a support group meeting. And when children used to attend these meetings, they would have cookies and sit quietly, but now girls as young as nine years old have been diagnosed with this disease and participate in the sharing.

Bodily Injury or Trauma

Some experts say that whole body trauma, neck injuries, and brain concussions from severe accidents, such as a car crash, can cause fibromyalgia. Some also distinguish posttraumatic FM from regular FM, while others point to an accumulation of provoking factors, with body trauma counting as a final provoking insult. It is not uncommon to see an accident victim going to physical therapy in the same building where he or she sees a pain management physician.

Emotional Trauma

Posttraumatic stress disorder, disorders of extreme stress, and severe psychological trauma as well as such emotionally brutal experiences as physical abuse, sexual molestation, rape, criminal assault, or violent combat in war have been linked to FM. These experiences make imprints on the brain that show up on functional brain imaging photographs. Moreover, these imprints do not diminish over years—they may be reactivated and vividly remembered years or even decades later. Some experts hypothesize that psychological trauma may help provoke or contribute to the onset of FM. Sometimes these painful memories are buried so deeply in the subconscious that a person needs professional help to face them. Emotional damage, when finally revealed, can be just as traumatic as the original event. We recommend caution and support when delving into these areas.

Infections That Affect Nervous Tissue and Brain Cells

Epstein-Barr virus, which is known for causing mononucleosis, and human herpesvirus-6 are examples of infections that affect nerves or brain cells that may have a connection to FM. Rigorous proof, however, is lacking, and research is needed to determine whether these infections really do play a role in causing FM.

Secondary Fibromyalgia

Secondary fibromyalgia is the term suggested for FM that is linked to other painful conditions. In these instances, the primary condition is not enough to explain the FM symptoms and findings. For example, rheumatoid arthritis is a primary condition in which FM may be found concurrently 25 percent of the time as a secondary condition. Secondary FM can be similarly diagnosed in 30 percent of patients who have lupus (systemic lupus erythematosus). Other conditions that may precede FM include chronic severe back pain and endometriosis. Whether any of these conditions are truly primary and trigger FM remains uncertain. Some of these related conditions are discussed again in Chapter 2.

THE GREAT PRETENDER

Even though there is a basic list of symptoms and causes, what makes FM different from other illnesses is that it is uniquely deceptive and difficult to diagnose. It is not a logical syndrome, and it is difficult to explain an illness with such diverse symptoms and such unpredictability.

The most shocking thing about having FM is that you may look absolutely normal—or even better than normal. It is almost a curse to retain your looks well into your eighties when every part of your body is run by a switchbox that sends out signals that make no sense at all. We are tempted to call this terrible syndrome "the great pretender" because people who have it hardly ever show it. It is not uncommon for those who suffer from chronic pain and illnesses like FM to take special care with their appearance to boost the spirits of other people around them. As a

WHY DO SOME PHYSICIANS REGARD FIBROMYALGIA WITH SUSPICION?

Fibromyalgia is sometimes regarded as an illegitimate illness simply because it cannot yet be fully explained. In 1990, the American College of Rheumatology, however, made a meticulous effort to substantiate the syndrome. The ACR first characterized the syndrome, then defined a homogeneous population of people with such a constellation of symptoms so that they could be studied rigorously to learn more about the disease and treat it. The criteria set up by the ACR for diagnosing FM are still in clinical use as they were set forth in 1990. Fibromyalgia has also found a place in major medical textbooks; *Harrison's Principles of Internal Medicine*, for example, began describing FM with an illustration of the eighteen tender points in its fifteenth edition (2001). As we have said earlier, all of these findings still do not provide a complete explanation. So, the debate surrounding FM's legitimacy will continue until the abnormalities in the nervous system circuits are fully elucidated and the triggers for the aberrations are well understood.

rule, many patients with severe pain really do appear outstandingly well because they have spent hours or even days preparing for that specific event. It is their time to be in the world, so they want to shine and enjoy it.

Besides experiencing physical pain that can rage violently one way or the other, FM patients also experience an emotional pain like no other—the pain of not being believed, accepted, and validated as a person who really has something physically wrong with you. Other people may have no idea what is going on in your life. To them, you look just fine, so why would you need medication, treatment, or any kind of special consideration? When you have had FM long enough, you can put on a good show by faking how you feel for a few hours before you collapse, but that does not mean you have a decent life. Your biggest struggle is trying to thrive in a world that thinks nothing is wrong with you!

Appearing so well and healthy also works against you in your relationships. Having an unseen chronic illness puts you in a difficult position because few people will ever know or really understand your situation. You are in double jeopardy trying to fight a physical disease along with all the emotional pain that comes with it—from not being understood! Fibromyalgia attacks your way of living as strongly as it does your body. The worst pain of FM is experiencing ruined careers, marriages, hopes, and dreams. The personal and social conflicts of having fibromyalgia or loving someone who has it are enormous and often overwhelming.

There is no cure for FM, but it can be medically managed to a certain degree. And your ability to adapt to the changes this hidden disease brings to your life is just as important as handling the physical symptoms. Now it is time to complete the picture by showing you exactly how to rebuild your life and your family relationships. After many years of experiencing these things, we would like to share solutions to the problems before you experience all of them. We have put together a four-step plan to help you manage the pain and learn to lead a fulfilling life again. If you follow these steps, you will have the power to rebuild your relationships and stabilize your stress. The key to this plan is learning how to restore yourself by learning new skills to protect your satisfying new lifestyle. This blueprint for dealing with and overcoming the struggles of FM has worked for many and our prayer is that it will bring you the same success. We will start by discussing various ways to receive the help you need to manage the pain of FM and then move into the Four Steps to Adaptation.

2

DIAGNOSING AND TREATING FIBROMYALGIA

⊙

Fibromyalgia remains elusive to diagnose despite guidelines published by the American College of Rheumatology in 1990. Therefore, symptoms (discussed in Chapter 1) can only suggest a diagnosis of the disease.

RULING OUT SIMILAR DISEASES

One of the challenges of diagnosing FM is that the presence of different disorders that resemble FM must be ruled out with blood tests and x-rays. For example, chronic pain all over can be seen in several spinal conditions and rheumatic disorders, such as lupus (systemic lupus erythematosus), PMR (polymyalgia rheumatica), and polymyositis. Ways to differentiate chronic fatigue syndrome, myofascial pain syndrome, and arthritis—other disorders that resemble FM—are discussed in the following sections.

Chronic Fatigue Syndrome (CFS)

The National Institutes of Health's criteria for diagnosing *chronic fatigue syndrome* cites fatigue of an unknown cause that persists or returns for more than six months. Overall, the primary difference between CFS and fibromyalgia lies in the unrelenting tiredness that CFS patients almost always fail to shake. Their fatigue is extreme and overwhelming, often described as malaise or a total lack of energy. In contrast, the most prominent feature of fibromyalgia is relentless pain of unknown origin that comes and goes without reason.

Myofascial Pain Syndrome

Traveling pain or *referred pain* means that when a particular point—a trigger point—is pressed, pain travels to another area of the body. *Myofascial pain syndrome* involves having these traveling pains in one area of the body, while fibromyalgia patients have these sensations in all four quadrants of the body. Myofascial pain commonly occurs in areas that are very problematic for FM people as well. However, only one trigger point needs to be present to be diagnosed with regional myofascial pain. Myofascial pain is often caused by injury, trauma, or extreme repetitive use of one part of your body, like grinding your teeth while sleeping. Temporomandibular joint pain dysfunction syndrome (TMJD) is probably the most common example of myofascial pain reported. The term *myofascial* comes from *myo-*, meaning *muscles*, and *fascia*, which is the thin layer of tissue covering, supporting, and separating muscles. This pain commonly occurs in the shoulder, neck, and upper torso area, but it can show up anywhere your body has been injured or overused.

Arthritis

There are over 100 types of arthritis. The common element among them is joint inflammation, which is when your own immune system attacks your body. The most common form of arthritis, degenerative joint disease, is the wear and tear of joints. It is not a problem of inflammation, and it is experienced by almost every FM patient. The major differences between arthritis and FM are that arthritis involves inflammation, possible damage and/or destruction to the joints, and with early diagnosis and treatment of arthritis you can help decrease further joint damage and control symptoms.

If you have FM, you may also have any number of overlapping illnesses or conditions, including rheumatic and autoimmune system disorders. Fibromyalgia by itself, however, is not destructive to joints in any way.

CONTROVERSIAL TOPICS AND SYNDROMES AND FIBROMYALGIA

Only time and continued research will deliver the answers to all of our questions about FM and what may or may not be related to it. Over the years, certain terms or phrases have come up suggesting a relationship between legitimate and unproven facts, and we discuss a few of them in the following sections. For a more in-depth resource on these controversial topics, we recommend that you read *Fibromyalgia: An Essential Guide for Patients and Their Families* by Daniel J. Wallace, M.D. and Janice Brock Wallace (available at fmaware.org). This book is an excellent medical/clinical presentation of FM and a quick read full of reliable medical information.

Lyme Disease

Lyme disease is a relatively uncommon condition caused by an infection from a bacterium that is spread through a tick bite. This disease was named for the area around Lyme, Connecticut, where it was first discovered, and it's characterized by several symptoms depending on the stage of infection. In early Lyme disease, within days to weeks of infection, patients can present with flu-like symptoms, fevers, joint and muscle pains, and a characteristic skin rash. In some patients, if left untreated for several months, the bacterium can spread and cause early disseminated disease, features of which can include neurologic and cardiac side effects. A small percentage of those patients whose disease remains untreated can develop a late disseminated form of the disease, characterized by an inflammatory arthritis usually in one or both knees. Luckily, depending on which stage of the disease is being treated, the bacterium is readily treated with common antibiotics. Almost all of these patients will be cured by eradication of the infection with antibiotics.

Some controversy exists regarding some patients who complain of symptoms such as pain, fatigue, and cognitive deficiencies that persist after their infection has been treated. Many of these symptoms resemble or may lead to development of fibromyalgia. However, most of the leading experts in this field do not believe that this "treatment-resistant" Lyme disease exists. Often, mention of the term *Lyme* raises eyebrows in medical circles because so much controversy, confusion, and misinformation about it has circulated within the fibromyalgia community over the years.

Reflex Sympathetic Dystrophy Syndrome

Reflex sympathetic dystrophy syndrome (RSDS) (or complex-regional pain syndrome) is a chronic pain syndrome that involves pain and swelling in affected limbs that is usually associated with "sympathetic" symptoms. Sympathetic symptoms can include swelling and edema, flushing, sweating, warmth or cooling, and loss of hair along the affected extremity. The condition can be triggered by a preceding trauma to the affected limb (such as jamming a toe or stepping on a nail) and can migrate to other regions of the body. Strokes are not uncommon precipitants of the condition. Many times, however, an antecedent cause cannot be found. Diagnostic testing can help suggest the diagnosis, and can include x-rays, bone scans, and surface temperature measurements of the arms and legs. Treatment includes use of pain relieving medicines, steroids, medicines used to treat neuropathy, and even intentional blockage of the inciting nerves.

The Role of Medicine in Managing Fibromyalgia

Although medical treatments do not eradicate fibromyalgia, they can help ease symptoms to more manageable levels. Medicine is a tool that helps, and to utilize this tool most effectively, you need medical information. This knowledge allows you and your family to be active participants in your care—an arrangement that will help you get the best care possible.

Team Approach to Medical Management

The medical treatment of FM usually employs a team approach involving healthcare practitioners from a variety of specialties. At present, no formal medical specialty exists that recognizes and works with FM and its related disorder, chronic fatigue syndrome. In his book on CFS and FM, *Tuning the Brain*, Jay A. Goldstein, M.D., has proposed a new specialty, called *neurosomatic medicine*. Until such a specialty takes off, FM authorities recommend recruiting a team of professionals to treat FM. Which professionals belong on your team?

Primary Care Physicians. A *primary care physician* (PCP)—an *internist, family physician,* or *ambulatory care physician*—performs several roles. One is to provide a portion of the care you need for FM and its multitude of symptoms. Another role is as a referral to appropriate specialists for such issues as pain management and overlapping conditions. Your primary care physician keeps up with your case by receiving feedback and reports from the specialists. He or she is the point person who coordinates your total care and helps you gather enough information to make the right choices; however, this physician is not responsible for your complete care. You are. Your primary care physician is also the one you depend on in case of emergencies like hospitalization.

Specialists. Your primary care physician may send you to a variety of specialists to help with various symptoms. One specialist is a *pain management consultant*, a physician who uses medicines and other techniques that apply to your symptoms to bring your pain to a more tolerable level. A *physical medicine and rehabilitation (PM&R) specialist* might also be called in as this specialty emphasizes muscle and skeletal disorders. Some, but not all, PM&R specialists work with FM patients.

A *rheumatologist* is an internist who specializes in treating arthritis and diseases of the joints. Most are very knowledgeable about FM and can be helpful in determining a diagnosis and recommending treatments, medications, and lifestyle changes to ease symptoms. It is also wise to see a rheumatologist to confirm whether any problems besides fibromyalgia are in play. Be alert for possible overlapping conditions.

Neurologists specialize in diseases of the brain and nervous system; they may be called in to help with neurological disorders distinct from FM. They can also be helpful in providing advice on the array of medications to manage pain. Many FM patients consult with a neurologist to rule out other difficulties that mimic FM and could be more serious, like multiple sclerosis.

Other team members include *counselors, physical therapists, occupational therapists, acupuncturists,* and *massage therapists*. Most primary care physicians recognize the helpfulness of counselors and can assist you in getting established with one. Physical therapists, acupuncturists, and massage therapists can help if they have experience working with FM patients.

In putting together your treatment team, remember that your mind, your body, and your spirit are more sensitive than those of the average person. Since stress and pain bother you more, make sure to find extra support in these areas. Also, be very cautious when anyone is physically touching your body or doing "hands on" work—be sure they understand how you differ from others and explain how their touch may affect your condition.

Choosing the Right Physicians

How do you find caring physicians, particularly primary care physicians, who do not sidestep the importance of a multi-disciplinary treatment approach to helping chronically ill patients? There is no substitute for searching and persisting. Check out your potential doctor in person and ask yourself: Does he or she answer my questions? Do I have a rapport with this physician? Will he or she give me the attention I need?

Do not stay with a physician who minimizes the need for pain control or full treatment of FM—transfer to another physician without guilt, embarrassment, or hesitation. Medicine cannot cure FM, but you want physicians who try their best to help you manage your symptoms. Find a medical partner that you are comfortable and confident with. See the discussion on Step Two (Chapter 4) for more information on this important decision.

CONTROLLING PAIN

Pain paralyzes action—if you live constantly in severe pain, you will get nowhere with your life or with adapting to fibromyalgia. To "tough it out" is not a virtue, it is stagnation. If medicine can bring your pain down to a tolerable level, then you can begin to take action. You might suppose that FM is a negligible illness and that it does not warrant taking medications. Nothing could be further from the truth. FM is a huge intrusion on normal living. Even if medicines do not eradicate the illness, if they partly restore your ability to function, they are worth taking.

Medicine is not the only tool for treating pain. For example, have you noticed that your pain changes in proportion to your stress level? Stress management is as important as medicine as a means of pain control. Nevertheless, medicine is a start. The sensible move is to create an optimal treatment using a combination of medicines, practices, and methods. Any treatment that makes a worthwhile contribution to your well-being is necessary for continued progress.

Who decides whether a medication is worthwhile for you? You should make precise reports to your physician, identifying which medications help and which do not, whether a dose has an effect, and so on. Keep notes and records of your symptoms and medicines for this purpose. It is difficult to predict your response to any medication unless you try it first, though we caution against taking any kind of medication merely on the advice of a friend. You need to test your tolerances by trial and error. Research the medicines prescribed since your doctor cannot teach you everything about them. In the end, you are the final arbiter regarding your medications. By trial and error, with your physician's help, you will ferret out which medications are effective.

Pain Medications

Medications can help you cope with most common symptoms of widespread pain and joint stiffness. Such medications include nonsteroidal anti-inflammatory drugs; mild analgesics, or painkillers; over-the-counter pain medications; muscle relaxants; antidepressants; opioids; and topical painkillers. When examining medications be sure to consider the benefits and risks of each group of drugs. Some of them are discussed in the following sections. It is important to talk with your doctor about the benefits and side effects of any medication that he or she is considering prescribing.

In addition to the physical risks, you may fear being stigmatized or labeled a drug addict for taking pain medication. We discuss this more in Chapter 4 in the section "Why People with Fibromyalgia Shun Medical Care" as well as in Chapter 5 in the section "Managing Pain with the Stigma of Fibromyalgia."

Nonsteroidal Anti-Inflammatory Drugs (NSAIDs). Common prescription NSAIDs include Feldene and Relafen. You may experience rashes, rapid heartbeat, stuffy nose, blurred vision, or lightheadedness when taking these types of drugs. In the extreme, they can cause gastritis—inflammation of the stomach—or ulcers in the stomach or small intestine. However, the primary side effect of these drugs is stomach upset, so take your medication with food. If necessary you might want to take over-the-counter medications, such as Tums or Rolaids. If you experience severe stomach pain, you should consult your doctor immediately. There are also over-the-counter drugs that can be used to treat pain, including the nonsteroidal agents aspirin and ibuprofen (Motrin or Advil).

The cortisone class of anti-inflammatory medication, such as Cortisol, Prednisone, Medrol, or Kenalog, is unlikely to bring relief because fibromyalgia is not an inflammatory condition. If you respond well to a medication of the cortisone class, your physician should reconsider the diagnosis of FM.

Mild analgesics include Ultram and Darvocet. Medications that are not officially analgesics, but that may help with pain, include Lioresol and Neurontin. Gabatril (pregabalin) has been released by the FDA, and several other soon-to-be-released medications may be useful for FM. In addition, several antidepressant medications may help you cope with pain (see Chapter 1).

Muscle Relaxants. These medications can help soothe muscle aches and pains. Flexeril is the most common of these drugs, but others include Zanaflex, Soma, Skelaxin, Baclofen, and Norflex. If you are taking muscle relaxants it is important that you do not take them with alcohol and that you avoid driving as these drugs can impair your ability to drive. Another side effect can be mild to severe gastrointestinal distress, which can include stomach pain or diarrhea. However, side effects depend on each individual's response to a particular drug, so even if you experience side effects on one medication, you may want to try another one to evaluate your response.

Narcotics. Opioid, or narcotic-like, medications can assist in your FM pain management—although the response varies from person to person. The only way to know whether they benefit you is to work with your physician on a trial basis. You may fear that in taking opioids you could become addicted to them. It may help you to know that the majority of patients take opioid medications for pain relief to live more functional lives. It is important to understand the difference between becoming tolerant to a medication as opposed to becoming addicted. When you take any medication, tolerance or physical dependence may occur as your body chemistry adjusts to the medicine. Make sure you know the drug's proper use and follow your doctor's instructions. Do not allow unreasonable fears to stop you from taking full doses of pain medication and miss the opportunity for at least some degree of relief. At the same time, in your relief to be moving around, be careful not to do too much in the beginning and make your symptoms worse from overexertion.

The warning on the prescription label, "Do not stop taking this medication without supervision of your physician" indicates that the drug you are taking cannot be stopped abruptly. You must taper off the medication according to a schedule to avoid coming off of it too quickly, which can cause severe side effects. Again, do not let the stigma of taking medication that you must go off of with caution deter you from using opioids for pain management.

Opiates offer many opportunities to help you regain a higher quality of living and functioning; however, opiates alone are not sufficient. Gauging, pacing, and managing your stress level all play a part in your improvement. When you finally experience some pain relief, you will quickly learn to not overexert yourself and lose the benefit of your new medication.

Opioid medication may be weak, moderate, or strong in effect. They come in both short-lasting (three- to four-hour) or long-acting (eight- to seventy-two-hour) kinds. For severe unremitting pain, most pain management specialists recommend long-acting opioids. To achieve twenty-four-hour control for chronic pain patients, many specialists rely on a combination of a long-acting, or controlled-release, medication and a short-acting, or quick breakthrough for an acute specific pain, medication.

For safe use, physicians warn you to never cut or break the time-release medications. However, it is often okay or even recommended to use a pill-cutter while adjusting to fast-acting medications. Patients can ask their pharmacy when they want to know if they should cut pills. In addition, some pills are "scored"—they have indentations so they are easier to cut.

Several new options in delivering opiate medication to the body are making "compassionate care" more easily attainable. For example, the Duragesic patch, which is applied externally, continuously delivers fentanyl through the skin into the bloodstream for up to seventy-two hours. This patch was introduced to the market for cancer patients and others who have difficulty swallowing medications. It has also proved helpful for people with gastrointestinal problems. Some physicians combine a low dose of the Duragesic patch along with a fast-acting painkiller like Lortab.

Another advance in delivering these medications has come through Actiq, an oral transmucosal form of the active ingredient in Duragesic, fentanyl citrate. Actiq is wrapped in individual doses on a stick similar to a lollipop; you rest the stick on the inside of your cheek to release the medication directly into the bloodstream. Both of these fentanyl products are extremely powerful medications that must be prescribed and carefully monitored by pain management specialists. Although they must be used with extreme caution, they can provide a tremendous level of pain relief.

You should know that a typical side effect of opiates is constipation. This is a manageable side effect that never goes away while on the medication. Side effects will go away once the drug is stopped; however, patients should be careful not to stop taking the medication too quickly to avoid withdrawal symptoms that are the opposite of their initial problem, such as diarrhea. Consider using over-the-counter treatments, such as magnesium oxide capsules; stool softeners, such as Docusate, Colace, Surfak; and bulking agents, such as Metamucil; and adding more fiber to your diet. Since opioids can produce a near-paralysis of the peristaltic movements of the bowel, additional over-the-counter colon stimulants, such as Dulcolax, Senna, and Sennakot, may be needed to overcome this side effect. Other laxative medications are available by prescription, so be sure to ask your physician about other options if necessary.

Sedation may be another side effect of opiates. To counter this, pain management physicians and rehabilitation specialists sometimes introduce small doses of methylphenidate (Ritalin) or other stimulants for patient trials. Several FM patients report that adding Ritalin allows them to tolerate the strong time-release pain medicines that allow them to get out of bed each day and compare the effect to having extra-strong coffee each morning. The only thing for certain in this area is that every patient responds differently to each medication, so it is critical to work closely with your physician. The issue comes down to finding out what is necessary to allow you to be as functional as possible.

Topical Painkilling Medications. Topical painkillers can be applied to hot spots—localized areas where pain is especially intense. For example, if you have neck pain or jaw pain that interferes with eating or grooming, it may be relieved with local painkillers. A prescription of Ketamine 10–15 percent in gel has been effective for this purpose. Other useful topical products include Ketoprofen gel (by prescription), Ultra Balm (over the counter), and Salon Pas Pain Patches (over the counter).

Nondrug Treatments for Pain

In addition to all of the medications available, there are many nonmedical treatments that can be used to help ease fibromyalgia pain. A variety of accessories, techniques, and self-help measures are available to help you cope with your symptoms. In addition to the following resources, you may also discover the benefits of heating pads, bandage wraps, and soothing pads that you can warm in the microwave and apply to your shoulders and other troubled spots.

Neurostimulators. An electric neurostimulator is a physical therapy device that can alleviate pain in regional muscle groups. Neurostimulators are similar to the older transcutaneous electric nerve stimulators (TENS units); however, neurostimulators apply the stimulation to the muscle tissue, not the skin (as in the TENS unit), providing an electrical massage to the muscle tissue as opposed to the skin irritation of the TENS unit to distract a patient from pain. Your physician can prescribe this device, and you can keep it permanently in your home. You may even be able to obtain one through your health insurance.

Self-Supervised Exercise Programs. Exercise is critical for maintaining your health and decreasing muscle pain. If you do not exercise, your muscles become tight and inflexible to the point where you may not be able to avoid hurting yourself. If possible, have a physical therapist custom-design an exercise program for you. If you need to design your own program, here are some things to get you started.

• Stretching and limbering routines: You can design a stretching program by following the pictures in such books as *The Arthritis Foundation's Guide to Good Living with Fibromyalgia*. You can also purchase videotapes showing stretching and limbering workouts from the Oregon Fibromyalgia Foundation website at myalgia.com.

• Pool exercises: Standing neck-high in a warm pool and moving body parts is considered by many FM experts as the premier form of self-supervised whole-body exercise. The water provides gentle resistance so that it is hard to injure your joints or muscles. Water also takes weight off of joints. Most gyms have warm pools (about 88 degrees) that can be used for this purpose, and in many locales, the Arthritis Foundation sponsors warm pool exercises. "Pool Exercise Program" is a video of forty-two Arthritis Foundation pool exercises that is available from online bookstores.

• Walking and treadmill exercise: If your hips, knees, ankles, and feet can handle ambulation, using a treadmill and walking are options. You can set your own intensity level and time limit so this exercise does not cause injury or post-exercise malaise.

• Low-impact floor exercises with music: In some areas, the Arthritis Foundation sponsors low-impact exercise classes. You can also purchase videotapes of FM exercises with music from the Oregon Fibromyalgia Foundation website at myalgia.com. Several levels of intensity are offered on these tapes, so you can choose the level that is right for you. Remember that muscle strain can occur if you exceed your capacity.

Be cautious about other forms of exercise unless you have the help of a physical therapist experienced with FM. Personal trainers at gyms seldom have a suitable background for helping people with FM. Physical therapists may be able to design aerobic exercises for you, but progress reaching higher heart rates takes extra time and you will need to be very cautious to avoid injuring your muscles or triggering post-exercise malaise. We also advise similar caution when using the Pilates method of body conditioning. With selection and modification, you can use some components of the Pilates method in an FM program. The assistance of a physical therapist to help you do this is invaluable.

Physical Therapy (PT). Physical therapists are trained in a large repertoire of techniques, but only some of those techniques work well for FM. It is essential to find a therapist familiar with FM and with the PT techniques that help it. A properly experienced therapist can offer you substantial help. Conversely, a therapist who does not understand FM can aggravate your symptoms.

Your physical therapist should have skills in manual techniques, or manual therapy. Examples of this include myofascial release, a highly specialized stretching technique used by physical therapists to treat patients with a variety of soft tissue problems, and strain–counter strain, a technique that involves shortening a muscle in spasm and allowing it to reset itself to a more normal state. Strain–counter strain is a very gentle technique that only requires you to relax while a therapist slowly moves some part of your body, depending on the location of your pain.

Your therapist should also work out an exercise program for you to do at home. These exercises stretch and strengthen muscles so that you can maintain the gains you have achieved and so that you are less likely to strain yourself in your daily activities. This therapeutic program should be individually designed and built around your needs. The therapist can design a home exercise program that uses a mat, a stretching band, and one-pound weights or an aquatic program for using in a warm pool.

Diet and Nutrition Supplements. So far no specific diet—such as a high- or low-carbohydrate diet—has been found to be helpful for the majority of FM people. However, a balanced diet that includes vegetables, fruit, and 100 percent whole fruit juices (for the minerals) is recommended. Adopt a health-building nutrition program suitable for your individual needs. Although many nutritional measures and supplements do not correct FM symptoms per se, they serve to promote general good health. We encourage you to take advantage of every means of building your health.

A magnesium supplement is highly recommended by many FM authorities and has been shown to decrease the tendency of muscles to hurt. The recommended daily dose is 400 mg, which is safe unless your kidneys have failed; an even larger dose may be helpful for some patients. A multivitamin supplement usually does not provide enough magnesium, so you will need a separate magnesium supplement to obtain the correct amount.

Make sure your calcium intake is adequate from two servings of milk per day or from 1200 mg in calcium supplements. Again, multivitamins contains less than the amount you need, so you will need a separate supplement if you do not obtain the calcium from milk. As for calcium from coral deposits, researchers recognize this as a source of calcium as long as it does not contain lead, but there is no advantage to this over other sources.

Natural Remedies and Herbs. One example of using natural remedies to ease FM symptoms is taking valerian root or kava extract to treat insomnia. These two substances can have a sedative effect. Be sure to discuss them with your physician if you wish to use them because they have side effects. For example, kava can cause liver damage and must be monitored with blood tests.

For the most part, natural treatments are unknown in their effectiveness and unproven in clinical trials. Research any natural treatment you intend to try in the Natural Medicines Comprehensive Database at naturaldatabase.com. This database has a comprehensive listing from all published clinical trials. Almost every natural treatment is listed. The database also explains any known side effects and is updated continually.

In addition to checking treatments in the database, avoid becoming fixated on this one track alone. Promoters of natural remedies are notorious for their excessive claims; make sure not to get derailed from your larger, more complete plan of care. Successful management of FM requires a broad attack; no single class of treatment suffices.

CONTROLLING SYMPTOM FLARE

You may experience fluctuations in the severity of your illness—up and down cycles—that are not caused by an identifiable factor. Symptoms may flare due to aggravating events, especially stress. And as powerful as pain medicine is, it can be offset by a stressful lifestyle. Lifestyle can be in constant clash with FM, so adjust your lifestyle to reduce stress and pain. Chapter 6 provides tips on managing stress, which is as essential for pain control as medication.

Another cause of symptom flare is due to you overexpending yourself. You will eventually learn how much energy you can expend before entering a flare. We provide time management and energy planning techniques in Chapter 5. Flu and other viral illnesses can cause a temporary flare of FM. Your symptoms may also flare after surgery, and your recovery time after surgery may be longer than for patients who don't have FM. Exposure to cold weather and changes in barometric pressure can also cause your symptoms to flare.

Physical care by itself is incomplete. The treatments listed in this chapter can decrease your symptoms of FM, but medical and physical remedies alone are rarely enough. And medications do not help you totally control pain. Gauging and pacing are also necessary, and stress reduction will further ease your pain. You need to create a lifestyle that accommodates FM and enables you to still live a fulfilling life.

It is abundantly clear that emotional care is essential to adequately control physical symptoms because the beneficial effects of medications can change in direct proportion to the level of stress in your life. Physicians frequently see FM patients who respond to medication but who suddenly crash when an emotional crisis arises. A patient not skilled in gauging and pacing is constantly cycling through overload followed by collapse.

Training in adapting and stress management helps reduce symptoms, yet an entire team of professionals cannot wholly solve the problems posed by FM. You and your loved ones are responsible for the quality of your life. We offer you this compendium of information to help you make steady strides toward a satisfying life.

3

STEP ONE: ASSESS YOUR REACTIONS TO FIBROMYALGIA

◉

Fibromyalgia is notorious for disrupting lives and families. The medical information in Chapter 2 shows that medications help but do not cure FM. You and your loved ones are left to deal with the life-altering impact of this illness—an enormous task! How do you rebuild a healthy pattern of living in the face of this illness? The answer is that you adapt; you take hold of this illness and actively construct a rewarding life despite FM. The huge process of adapting can be organized into a series of tasks. By proceeding systematically, you can make steady progress. Tackled individually, no task is overpowering.

The life work of adapting begins in the only place it can: exactly where you are now. It begins with your initial reactions to FM. This is the starting place for both you and your loved ones. To move forward, you need to know precisely where you are and what you are dealing with.

In this chapter, we will describe the most common reactions to having FM. As you read through these reactions, you will recognize the ones that apply to you. It is by assessing these reactions that you can learn to accept your situation and start improving the quality of your life. Even if you are in a terrible place emotionally, let us assure you that difficult starting points are not unusual. After you have started, you will persevere to find success in a matter of time. By assessing your current position, you can orient yourself and embark on a life-changing journey.

Identifying Your Reactions to Fibromyalgia

Read this chapter and mark the sections that describe your reactions to FM; you can skip over the reactions that don't apply to you. We use the term *reactions* in the plural because you and your loved ones will probably have more than one reaction to FM. All your reactions are important and merit attention. Increasing your awareness of your emotions strengthens your insight into your present condition. After you have assessed which reactions apply to you, you will find details and strategies on how to resolve them in the second half of the chapter.

Reaction One: Denial

Have you found yourself wanting to deny the reality of your situation, thinking that your fibromyalgia may go away on its own? Do you just wish your FM would take care of itself? This reaction is typical of denial, or nonacceptance of your situation. As your symptoms continue to get worse, you will have no choice but to seek out medical care. You may have already seen several doctors and begun to suspect what is really going on. Possibly you've consulted several doctors before you received a definite diagnosis of FM. Maybe a friend suspected the diagnosis and a doctor confirmed it. However you discovered what was going on; just knowing the truth can be important and reassuring. A definite answer brings some relief because now you know that your pain is real and that you are not crazy. The relief may be short-lived, however, when you learn that FM is a painful, fatiguing, and chronic illness and that medical science has not found a cure.

Denial can be mild, moderate, or overwhelming. It may be blind to one area but not others and can include:

• The reality of the diagnosis

• The permanency of the illness

• The need for treatment

- Your identity as a person with FM

- Minimization of symptoms, including pain

Your symptoms may be overpowering to deal with, but by ignoring them you are only deceiving yourself and everyone else. Pain and fatigue may be wrecking your normal pattern of life, but you are downplaying it and pushing yourself on. By not listening to your body, you are setting yourself up for a cycle of collapse that surely won't allow you to lead a satisfying life. Yet, even after a collapse, you may continue to tell yourself that it isn't real and get right back up again.

How do you get out of denial? You need some form of a reality check, which will probably come after a terrible ordeal of suffering. You need to understand what the illness is and what it is doing to you before it gets worse. So, now that you finally acknowledge that you have fibromyalgia, what is next? You might be angry and still protest furiously about having an incurable illness. You may be outraged: why me? These reactions are part of the grieving process, which is discussed more fully later in this chapter. After your anger cools down, you will need to find out what the raw reality of FM is. Answering these questions will bring you close to an accurate appraisal of your situation so you know where you stand.

Reaction Two: Denial on the Part of Loved Ones

Some loved ones react with extraordinary insight and care, rushing to the side of their partner to assist, console, and support. If you are one of these compassionate people, you may already know someone with FM, so you are able to recognize the situation quickly, or perhaps a loved one of yours is or was suffering from a chronic illness, so you are prepared for your spouse's denial. In either case, you are ahead of your spouse in accepting the reality of the situation and you can help her or him through it.

For most supporters, FM in your spouse seems out of place because it seldom shows itself clearly as a visible infirmity. You yearn for your partner to be healthy, so you may reject the idea that he or she has pain and illness. There are two major reasons why you might doubt your spouse's illness. First, the universal human tendency is to ignore unwanted intrusions on daily living. No caring spouse wants his or her partner to have chronic illness. The second reason for doubt is derived from society's faultfinding stance, for we take our cues from the culture in which we are immersed. The tendency of society is to view people with invisible pain as being "sickly" or otherwise deficient or flawed. At its worst, this societal attitude challenges the worth of the FM sufferer with scorching invalidations, implying that he or she can't really be that sick and they need to toughen up. This cold attitude occurs with virtually every chronic illness, more so with invisible illnesses—illnesses with no orthotic devices, deformities, or signs of physical infirmity. For more information about society's attitude toward chronically ill people, read *Life with Chronic Illness: Social and Psychological Dimensions* by Ariela Royer.

You may have doubts and are searching for ways to verify that your loved one is suffering from a real illness. However, someone else's opinion won't suffice to give you the assurance you are looking for. Keen observation on your part is needed. Some things you can do to help with your assessment and your capacity to tune into your spouse's illness include:

• Research the medical information on fibromyalgia. Look over the first few chapters in this book. Another resource is *Validate Your Pain* by Allan Chino, Ph.D., and Corinne Davis, M.D. Note the descriptions of symptoms and findings of people with FM and compare them to those of your partner.

• Observe your loved one's symptoms. Are your partner's bodily movements the same as when he or she felt well? Do they differ from other people who feel well? Gauge the level of pain your spouse is experiencing. Is she putting on a false front of cheerfulness while living in pain? Is he overdoing himself? Can you predict collapses?

• Watch for other symptoms of fibromyalgia. Are the symptoms you observe now different from the symptoms at another time? Gently massage some of his or her main muscle groups. How taut are they compared to times when they felt well? You may want to be aware of this so you know when you need to offer more assistance and support.

• Accompany your loved one on doctor visits. What your spouse says about him- or herself to a doctor will seldom be what he or she says to you and your family. The doctor may discuss FM or answer questions about your spouse, and you can then learn new things about what he or she is experiencing.

• Observe other people who have fibromyalgia. It can be quite valuable to meet other people with FM. To find a support group near you, go online to fmaware.org and click on "support group directory." If a local support group is not available, you may need to ask around to find other families affected by FM in your area.

• Observe friends and acquaintances, relatives and nonrelatives, young and old people with chronic illness. What are their struggles? In what ways do their difficulties resemble your loved one's struggles? You may want to be more observant of people in general to heighten your awareness as to how your loved ones are doing.

• Identify your loved one's reactions to fibromyalgia as described in this chapter. Every chapter in this book has information that is useful for people who are supporting FM patients. Each of the Four Steps to Adaptation involves work specifically for loved ones.

Reaction Three: Supernormalizing or The "Superwoman" Reaction

Fibromyalgia may not strike you suddenly, stopping you in your tracks. You may have noticed symptoms accumulating as time goes by. Have you tried to carry on as though you are not ill? Have you defied the illness by overcompensating, using every ounce of energy you have? Have you turned on the afterburners to prove to yourself and onlookers that FM cannot deter you? If so, you are responding to FM with the supernormal reaction, which is when you refuse to make adjustments for FM and to let FM slow you down.

People with FM have a tendency to run at high speed until fatigue and pain make it impossible. In doing so, nobody can accuse them of easily caving in or lazily giving up without a fight. *Supernormalizing*, so termed by Ariela Royer, is defiance of incapacity, a proclamation that you are unaffected by ill health despite worsening symptoms. It is a demonstration to yourself and to others that you are every bit as good as you ever were. If you're a mother, for example, it might mean a schedule of running your children to activities, doing housework, shopping, and attending meetings as well as working full-time. This lifestyle would wear anyone into the ground soon enough; but in a person with FM, it has serious consequences.

To attempt to be supernormal is to mismanage your illness, and the repercussions can come in various forms. You may experience a pattern of alternating collapses and recoveries because you go like fury until you collapse physically and mentally and are forced to rest and recover. Or you may steadily spiral down toward a major setback. The eventual cost for mismanaging FM includes:

- Worsening pain

- Increasing fatigue

- Feelings of despair

- Forfeiture of your physical and emotional health

- Recurring setbacks and losses in your ability to function

The attempt to be supernormal is not compatible with building a satisfying life, and you'll need to eventually accept your situation if you want to return to some semblance of your previous way of life.

Reaction Four: Damage to Your Sense of Self-Worth

What has FM subtracted from your sense of self? Perhaps formerly you were active, productive, outgoing, reliable, diligent, attentive, and emotionally steady. New traits, such as pain, fatigue, forgetfulness, breathlessness, and mood swings, that arrive in the FM package are often unwelcome and demean your feelings of worthiness. Has FM damaged your social identity? You might feel inferior because of your lessened ability to be involved in social activities. Your acquaintances may view you as someone with an infirmity who can never function like they do. Their reactions may be partly concealed or obvious and unpleasant and may harm your sense of self-worth.

A blow to your self-worth can also come from your belief systems. You may feel ruined and question whether you did something to deserve this fate. Or you may think that life has not been fair, that you've barely begun your life and already it is "over." Illness can destroy careers and make people financially dependent on others—the repercussions of which can be detrimental to your sense of self-worth. Refer to Chapter 5 for how to repair damage to your sense of self-worth.

Reaction Five: Guilt

Life with FM can create tremendous feelings of guilt. For example, have you felt so stiff and painful in the morning that it is hard to get moving and prepare breakfast for your family? If so, and you feel bad about it you may feel a sense of guilt. But why should you feel any guilt when the illness came uninvited? You did not do anything wrong, and you cannot be held responsible for bringing FM onto yourself. Maybe you had been employed and earned part of your family's income but then lost your job because of FM. You may feel devastated and think that it is your fault that your family is on such a tight budget. Do you feel guilt over your inability to function in your regular roles? Family expectations, if not adjusted to meet the new realities of fibromyalgia, can make you feel guilty.

The culture in the United States is intolerant of people who do not carry out their obligations or pull their share of the load. Blame is dished out rapidly and liberally for slacking off. You may hear people questioning the validity of your illness because you seem reasonably healthy. As a result, you may find yourself accused of trying to sneak out without doing your work. You may even agree and feel guilty for your inability to do your work. After all, you easily did these things in the past, and none of your obligations have changed. The presence of guilt may seem out of place, but it is the fact of the situation.

Reaction Six: The Frenzied Search

The frenzied search can occur when you staunchly refuse to accept that FM is incurable, or it may happen when your partner refuses to accept that adjustment for FM is necessary. You and your partner may refuse to let FM interfere with your plans or your marriage, telling each other that you must get rid of FM before it ruins your life together. Despite your defiant posture, however, FM starts to interfere with many kinds of activities. You and your partner react to these impositions, agreeing that something must be done immediately. Thus, you conclude that there has to be an answer to this problem and that you both will search until you find it, resulting in a frenzied search for solutions. The frenzied search reaction causes injury mainly for two reasons: first, the search may result in costly, unnecessary, or sometimes damaging treatments; and second, you cannot make progress in adapting during a frenzied search because your frenzied emotional state works against FM.

The frenzied search leaves no stone unturned. When one doctor or treatment does not produce rapid results, you move on to another, until you've been to ten doctors, none of whom has done anything for you. Maybe these ten doctors are not doing their job, but more than likely this represents a frenzied search. If these are competent doctors, they are probably not giving you the answers you were hoping to hear. You don't want to hear that FM can be treated but not cured and that symptoms can usually be managed but not eradicated. It's unacceptable to you that this is a new way of life that requires patience and cooperation.

So you continue your search and avoid adapting. You desperately pursue any leads: from friends, websites, ads, paid commercials, and FM conferences. A myriad of unscrupulous treatments are touted, and as a frenzied searcher, you are a juicy target for promoters. Sometimes your search leads you into expensive herbal and nutritional products, detoxification programs, elimination diets, hormone regimens, or intravenous vitamins. You may find elaborate treatments for yeast infections, intestinal microorganisms, and how to avoid exposure to unusual bacteria. In desperation, you may go to a big-name medical center to get the million-dollar diagnostic work-up—which usually turns up little more than a confirmation of the original diagnosis. You may even attempt treatments that turn out to be damaging—challenging workout programs, Rolfing, various surgeries, or even suddenly stop taking prescribed medications.

Keeping an eye out for promising new treatments is different from making a frenzied search. We recommend a practical and diligent search, not a frenzied one.

Reaction Seven: Grief from Good-bye Losses

Good-bye losses are the types of losses in which things you previously had in your life are gone, or when your close friends or family members move away or die. Good-bye losses for the FM sufferer might include the end of:

• Participating in sports like tennis and skiing

• Late nights out on the town

- Relationships with friends who reject people with chronic illness

- Strenuous travel

- An active life of almost any sort

- Intense career or job

- Financial security

The good-bye losses for the support person can also be extensive and can include:

- Decreased level of social activity, recreation and hobbies, lifestyle, and emotional satisfaction

- Less affection due to the effects of FM on your loved one's mood

- Decreased sexual contact due to your partner's pain or lack of desire

- Loss of financial security due to loss of an income

- Reduction in free time due to increased responsibilities

As you read, both you and your loved one should begin taking inventory of your losses. The list will come in handy as you work to resolve these issues in your new way of life. Social losses are often staggering once FM restricts your activities. Your friends may react in unexpected ways. People you considered to be loyal may begin to show intolerance toward your chronic illness. A friend may have only liked your companionship for activities that you can no longer do. You need to be prepared for a strong possibility that many of these people could desert you.

You may also encounter losses in your family relationships. We all expect our relatives to be more loyal than anyone in our social circles, but you may be surprised to find that some of them are quick to flee because they also find FM to difficult to accept. In your immediate family, there may be a sense of loss over the breakdown of the family's system of living. The accustomed roles—who takes care of the chores, the children, the bills, the shopping, and the cooking—may be disrupted for a time. Most importantly, the delicate balance of giving and receiving satisfaction and comfort among you and your loved ones may be changed.

The normal, human, and appropriate response to such losses is to grieve or to mourn. Most of the information and research we have on grief refers to bereavement, or grieving the death of someone close. However, the mourning process also applies to losses incurred by FM. Resolution and closure can be reached by going through the stages of the mourning process, which we discuss in a later section in this chapter, "Resolution of Good-bye Losses."

Reaction Eight: Resignation over Hello Losses

Resolving your grief over your good-bye losses is only part of the process. FM is doubly troublesome because of another dimension of loss, *hello losses*. Hello losses are the shocking realization that new challenges have arrived at your doorstep. You are saying hello to the new you, the one who lives every day with pain, fatigue, and other symptoms and who is not able to live much of the life you are accustomed to. These losses may include:

- Fatigue and pain that are worsened by exertion

- A tendency to be more easily emotionally distressed than before

- A decreased ability to push yourself, to work harder, or to concentrate as intensely as you used to

Unlike the good-bye losses, you do not bid hello losses adieu and put them away in a peaceful, restful place. They actively accompany you in daily life. You may experience grief when you recognize that hello losses are permanent. Grief is appropriate, but you cannot resolve hello losses by the mourning process. You may attempt to accept hello losses, but mere acceptance can easily drift into demoralization, resignation, despair, or a sense of helplessness.

To resolve a permanent ongoing loss you need to confront FM and adapt to it. By doing so, you look not only at hello losses but also to the future. You envision the accomplishments that will bring you closer to a fulfilling life despite FM and you move forward by resolving both good-bye and hello losses. To neglect either type of loss will hamper your forward progress.

RESOLVING YOUR INITIAL
REACTIONS TO FM

To resolve your initial reactions and move through Step One of adaptation, follow the procedure in this section. If you have not already done so, list all of your reactions to FM and do a full assessment of them. Neither you nor your loved one will be able to move past your initial reactions without first recognizing that they exist and then fully understanding them. Completely assessing your reactions gives you a penetrating view of how this illness is affecting your life and is a powerful means of stripping away misperceptions.

Next, make a list of the losses you have incurred from FM. You now have two lists: a list of reactions and a list of losses. You and your partner's lists will most likely be different.

After you have identified your reactions and losses, ask yourself: Are my reactions permanent, or can I get rid of them? Are my losses permanent, or can I get rid of them, too? We believe that you can get rid of reactions—by clarifying and understanding them so that you can see through and dissolve them. Many losses, however, are permanent. Treatment may ease your symptoms to a degree, but med-

---

SAMPLE LIST OF REACTIONS AND LOSSES FOR PEOPLE WITH FM

Reactions

- Denial: "It's only a phase. I just need rest and then I'll be up to speed."
- Guilt: "I feel terrible because I can't keep up with things like cooking and cleaning the house."
- Resentment: "What's going on? I've never felt or acted like this before. This is not like me at all!"

Losses

- Social activities: Staying out late with my friends on Saturday nights
- Previous job or career: Had to quit job because pain and symptom flares were preventing me from working long hours
- Health: Pain, fatigue, IBS, lack of sleep, overall discomfort
- Activities: Can no longer play tennis, go jogging, or play outside with my kids

---

Sample List of Reactions and Losses for the Loved One

Reactions to FM

- Denial and misunderstanding: "At first, I actually didn't believe that she was in pain—she just didn't seem sick."
- Frenzied search: "There has to be an answer to this problem, and I will search until I find it."

Losses Sustained

- Companionship, social activity, and recreational activity: "We used to go jogging together. We no longer go to parties together, or enjoy going to the movies on the weekends."
- Family income: "She had to quit her job so now we're living on one income."
- Family roles: "I have to do twice as many chores around the house as I used to."

---

icine has not cured FM. Therefore, your symptoms remain along with the losses you incur due to your symptoms.

By appraisal and persistence, you can discard your initial reactions to receiving a diagnosis of FM and start anew.

- If your reaction is denial, your appraisal allows you to acknowledge FM, its pain, its fatigue, and your lost pattern of living. Your losses remain, but the denial is gone.

- If your reaction is guilt, your appraisal shows you that no one is at fault for the symptoms of FM or the loss of your ability to carry out roles. Your losses remain, but you let go of the guilt.

- If your reaction is to supernormalize, your appraisal shows that your attempts to maintain normalcy at the cost of your health have to be stopped, although the symptoms of FM remain.

- If your reaction is a loss of your sense of self-worth, refer to Chapter 5 where we discuss ways to build it back up. The losses remain, but you can deal with them directly.

After seeing through your reactions, discard them. Acknowledge both your hello and good-bye losses. The brunt of your task now falls to dealing with these losses. We will address them one at a time, first the good-bye losses, then the hello losses.

RESOLVING YOUR GOOD-BYE LOSSES: ACCEPTANCE WITH COMPOSURE

Once your reactions to fibromyalgia are out of the way, your task becomes dealing with your losses. The two categories of losses need to be handled separately. We start with good-bye losses, which you may resolve through the mourning process. You may be avoiding activities you once loved to do, because it is depressing to think about it. Your grief here is over the loss of formerly enjoyed activities. By perpetually avoiding these memories, however, you will remain inwardly sad and resentful about what life has dished out. You will not reach closure until you resolve them.

Applying the Stages of Grief to Resolve Good-bye Losses

Look at the stages of grief, which were first set forth by Elisabeth Kübler-Ross, M.D., and described by other researchers. As we list them below, we will substitute good-bye losses due to FM for losses due to death and then apply these stages to working through Step One of the adaptation process.

1. Denial: Denying that you have FM and that FM is permanent.
2. Anger: Feeling anger that includes resentment, self-blame, and being cheated by life.
3. Bargaining: Thinking that if you straighten up and do right, your losses will be restored.
4. Depression: Feeling the grief and depression that comes with realizing that the loss is irretrievable.
5. Acceptance: Accepting this illness and the losses you have incurred from it.

Working Through the Mourning Process

The mourning process is described by William Worden, Ph.D., in *Grief Counseling and Grief Therapy* and it includes a sequence of tasks that apply to adapting to FM.

• Task One: Accept the reality of your loss. Your first step is to get a grip on the fact that you have a chronic illness and you won't be the same. Before you move to Task Two you need to accept the reality of your situation or it will be impossible to take the next step. Some patients need time to themselves to just sit with it. Other patients surround themselves with loved ones to discuss the situation.

• Task Two: Work through the grief. Psychologists consider it necessary for people to feel the pangs of grief before they can feel release. Let yourself experience the emotional responses from Kübler-Ross's stages of grief: anger, bargaining, and depression. Dr. Worden's research makes it clear that all people struggle in their dealings with grief but that some individuals encounter extreme difficulty with this task. He identifies factors that interfere with the successful completion of mourning, including the degree of the person's attachment to the losses, the person's ability to handle reversals, and a crisis of faith. For many, these are major issues that need to be settled before coming to terms with FM.

• Task Three: Adjust to an environment in which your old way of life and previous friends are missing. This task can be huge if you are facing FM. It might mean finding a new job because you lost your old one and finding new friends who will accept your illness. It could mean revamping family roles so that your family still enjoys doing things together. The response to losses due to FM is frequently inaction instead of adjustment. Instead of finding suitable employment to replace the old job, you may accept prolonged unemployment. Instead of seeking out new friends, you may settle for no friends. Family roles may not be restructured; instead, your family may do nothing to find fulfillment. An important part of resolving your past is to find new patterns and replacements for the things you have lost. We discuss rebuilding these patterns in your life in Chapter 5.

• Task Four: Emotionally relocate the losses and move on with your life. According to Dr. Worden, it is not necessary to purge yourself of every trace, feeling, and memory of your treasured past. Instead, you can move the memories to another place. For example, if you lose a job, you can move a portion of those previous job skills to the present and put them to use rather than forgetting and discarding them. Alternatively, you can memorize your previous job accomplishments and remember them fondly in the present.

The final resolution of good-bye losses is acceptance with composure—without bitterness, cynicism, resentment, or regret. To do this brings closure to your good-bye losses and gives you the ability to move forward.

RESOLVING HELLO LOSSES: DETERMINATION TO ADAPT

As we have already noted, losses that stay with you permanently are not going to be resolved by mourning over them. Because hello losses persist every day, your grief and mourning would never end and would lead to continual sorrow, demoralization, and resignation. You need to proactively rebuild your new life, and for this, you need vigorous action. While you may receive advice from all directions, do not let it deflect you off your course because handling FM requires broad-scale adjustments.

Once you have removed outside influences, examine your prospects in private. What action can you take? Is there more than one option? Envision the quality of life that you can achieve by finding the right care, support groups, medications, therapy, and stress reduction workshops to support you.

You can find future possibilities and tools throughout this book to use to create a fulfilling lifestyle. Look for inspiration from people who have succeeded in adapting. You may know someone personally, perhaps at a support group, who is an inspiration to you in this manner. After you have reviewed your prospects and envisioned your future, make your own decision. Ignite your determination and move forward to Step Two.

4

Step Two: Take Responsibility for Finding Care and Learning to Adapt

◉

Welcome to Step Two! Take a quick glance back to review what you have accomplished at Step One. You have taken stock of the many ways FM has affected your life. You have surveyed your options and your prospects for achieving a rewarding life. Doing this much hopefully has invigorated your pursuit of beneficial goals. The Step One tasks were necessary to give you determination to take vigorous action. (If you feel your determination cooling down now and then, review Step One to reenergize yourself.) Now, looking forward to the upcoming tasks, you can start to anticipate a successful journey.

The Components of Comprehensive Care

To rebuild your life, you will need to take responsibility for surrounding yourself with comprehensive care, including physical and emotional care, and acquiring adaptive training in all domains of your life. You will also be responsible for contracting out some of the work to be done; for example, you will find specific health-care providers to perform specialized services for you.

- Physical care: You will need proper physical care both at home and from health-care providers. Home care includes sound and regular sleep; proper nutrition; regular exercise, such as stretching and limbering exercises, pool exercises, low-impact exercises, and custom-designed home exercises; adjustment of family roles; and health-promoting practices in general. Medical care includes help from a multidisciplinary medical team—a primary care physician, a pain management physician, a physical medicine and rehabilitation specialist, and a physical therapist. Others may also be needed.

• Emotional care: You may need personal care unique to your life situation. Counseling and support groups are some options. It also may be necessary for you to deal with emotional difficulties due to losses, blocks, and traps. See Chapter 7 for more information.

• Adaptive training: Adaptive training enables you to implement the Four Steps to de-stress all of the domains of your life: self-worth; energy and resources; family life; relationship with your spouse, friends, relatives, and social circle; and your job, career, or business. Adaptive training helps you handle the stress and crises that threaten your progress.

Finding Comprehensive Care and Adaptive Training

To acquire adequate adaptive skills and to ensure that you obtain comprehensive care, you may have to search for competent help. Dealing with this illness alone will not work. The training you need is broad in scope, so you will need information from all available sources including those listed here.

• Books and articles: Read anything you can find on adapting to illness. Go to the library and request all the information they have on the topic. At online bookstores, search for books keyed under "psychology of chronic illness." Tapes and books on stress management also can be helpful.

• Adaptive training seminars: A clearinghouse for adaptive training seminars can be found online at the website fmadapt.com. Stress management seminars can also help you.

• Professionals: Properly selected professionals can provide the right kind of training. Specifically, medical family therapists who have a background in fibromyalgia, but general family therapists who are familiar with chronic illness are also quali-fied. Clinical psychologists specializing in health psychology or pain psychology as well as clinical psychologists familiar with chronic illness also should have the knowledge and experience you need. It's important to find a professional who is familiar with helping people adapt to chronic illness.

Overcoming Obstacles to Getting Care and Adaptive Training

The barriers to seeking adaptive training and getting comprehensive care can be numerous, but this section should help you identify and dismantle them. By the end of this chapter, no obstacle will deter you, and you will be able to move forward with unflinching decisiveness.

Denial and Postponement. Have you thought that your achiness and fatigue were just temporary phases that you would get over soon? This response is a typical exam-ple of denial. While you might realize that fibromyalgia is not a temporary condi-tion, you are still incorrectly hoping that next year will bring relief. As a result, you have ultimately failed to accept the reality of FM. Without a firm understanding of this illness, neither you nor your family can begin to progress because you will not seek out adaptive training. If you find that you or your loved ones haven't accepted that you have a chronic illness, refer back to Chapter 3. You still have work to do on Step One.

Failure to Take a Comprehensive Approach. Success in only a few tasks and treat-ment of only one type are not enough to help you cope with FM. To miss any main component of care compromises your chances for a satisfying adaptation. Remem-ber, FM is an illness that is not curable; it is treatable, but not by medicine alone. If one single remedy, such as nutrition, exercise, or pain medicine, or approach, such as positive thinking or healing energy, could "cure" FM, it would appear on the cover of *Newsweek*.

To attain your wanted lifestyle, you and your loved one must take advantage of every possible avenue that can help you. Getting stuck on a single approach or treat-ment is a typical obstacle to adaptation that will slow down your progress signifi-cantly. The most commonly omitted component of care is the social—or emotional—part. Adapting emotionally and socially is more difficult than taking care of physical needs, so make sure to pay close attention to you and your loved one's emotional needs.

Reluctance About Receiving Care at Home. To reconstruct a life pattern, you must not be hesitant about receiving help from your family. Your aim is the best family life possible, and this will determine much about the character of your social life and work environment. To reach a fulfilling lifestyle, your family's involvement is necessary. Once your own family members realize the need to pitch in and be supportive, they usually do just that. They may set up caregiving roles with various jobs assigned to different family members. Each assumes a portion of the responsibility for carrying out the new goals.

The most common obstacle is the FM person's refusal or hesitation to receive help. The very thought of depending on help from others, including family members, may be loathsome, and you may avoid it unless it is absolutely necessary. Even then, you may talk negatively to yourself about needing the help. Stop that. We all need help sometimes and you deserve it. Your personal views on independence versus interdependence may come into question, but you need to let it go. Refusing help—giving up some of your independence—is in opposition to your goal of adapting, and you need to reassess your values. Your family will probably find great satisfaction in sharing and distributing responsibilities. At the same time, however, the new family roles should not deprive you of all your former roles. You can retain many helpful roles as long as they don't compromise your health. Step Three (see Chapter 5) lists the tasks to setting up and developing new roles.

Misplaced Responsibility for Care. Your skills and involvement in organizing a team of comprehensive care-givers are critical for achieving life success. You and your family are in the position to monitor your total care, to make sure your progress does not get mired down, and to see the entire picture. Taking responsibility for success depends on you for several reasons:

- FM has disrupted your previously satisfactory lifestyle and is here to stay

- You and your family are faced with rebuilding a life pattern, one that will bring fulfillment

- No one else will take full responsibility; if you are going to receive complete care, you must take charge

WHY PEOPLE WITH FIBROMYALGIA SHUN MEDICAL CARE

Many people who have been unquestionably diagnosed with FM avoid medical care by their own choice. We polled our support groups to find out why. Our first finding was that many FM sufferers are still struggling at Step One. They have not yet acknowledged the new reality of FM or their need for receiving complete care. Those who are not finished with Step One tend to view medical care as an unwelcome intrusion forced on them, not as a means to reach their goal for a quality life. They are therefore unwilling to pursue long-term objectives. Instead, they accept only the minimum of treatment, hoping the illness will soon pass, but find that this approach doesn't provide a fulfilling, rewarding life.

An even more surprising discovery was that some people with FM recognize that they have a life-altering illness but refuse medical care anyway. Some of them avoid going to doctors or taking medication because they don't want to be seen as whiners and complainers. They refuse treatment because other FM people take medication for every symptom or use illness as a means to gain attention and sympathy. Many of these FM people stoically endure their symptoms and live shut-in or near-reclusive lives.

Other people with FM said they only use natural remedies and would only take drugs if it was absolutely unavoidable. Natural treatments and pharmaceutical treatments are not mutually exclusive. Natural remedies, such as magnesium, can contribute to health and FM management, but they cannot replace medical treatment or be used to the exclusion of medication. While promoters of natural treatments may disparage medical treatments and some may believe that natural treatments provide what is needed as well as medicine, it is important to seek out all legitimate sources of help, including medications.

Other patients answered that they avoid medical treatment out of fear of becoming a "zombie" or an "addict." The long lists of side effects issued with every prescription at the pharmacy cause many people to blanch. Looking at these lists, a person could easily conclude that all medications are more dangerous than helpful. However, it is the patient's responsibility to tell the prescribing physician when he or she feels a zombie-like or other negative side effect. Medication typically requires adjustment over several office visits. It is a good idea to keep a notebook of medications tried and adverse effects experienced.

Addiction to pain medication in people who have never been addicts is not likely to occur. Few people experience mood elevation states ("buzz" or "high") on medication. People who manipulate doctors to obtain prescriptions to get high are addicts. The majority of pain patients on painkillers are not addicts. Medical pain management can result in tolerance or physical dependence on medication. Tolerance is a commonplace occurrence and is not the same as addiction.

Unfortunately, many of us incorrectly assume that a specialist—or the health-care system in general—will take full charge of a medical condition and provide the best care possible. For acute conditions such as pneumonia or a fractured wrist, the medical profession does fairly well at providing complete care—but not for FM or chronic conditions. No single physician specializes in the entire spectrum that comprises fibromyalgia. Professionals assume responsibility within the confines of their specialty. Their help can be potent within a narrow scope, but it is not complete. Medical specialization does not address all aspects of an illness like FM, and medical professionals seldom take on their patients' total care.

If you do assign full responsibility for your care to only one doctor, you may find that your progress is slow to improve. Physicians and counselors can help with differing areas of care. But you and your family need to attend to your complete treatment plan.

Reluctance About Receiving Professional Care. Reluctance can get in the way of adaptive training for social and emotional care as well as medical care. It is surprising that FM sufferers and their families shun health-care professionals in a society that values technical competence. On the surface, it seems easy—you just reach for the telephone and call for an appointment. But in fact, most people with FM refuse professional care, so much so that most of them have inadequate care.

Procuring the Physical Care You Need

As discussed in earlier chapters, recognition of fibromyalgia as a legitimate medical illness has come about slowly. Nevertheless, FM is fully recognized in standard textbooks, and there is no excuse for a physician to undertreat or disregard your symptoms. Because this society tends not to validate people with chronic illness it will be your responsibility to advocate for yourself. Given the current health-care climate, this section provides some recommendations for surrounding yourself with the right professional care. It's in your best interest to be an active and informed participant in your own care; to do so you need to know about possible treatments that may be helpful to you. Many effective treatments for various FM symptoms are listed in Chapter 2. If you feel that your doctors are way off track in their approach to FM, do not try to educate them—find a new doctor. Your job is to search out the care you need, not to reform society. At the same time, however, be realistic in your expectations. Physicians today are not able to cure or eradicate FM symptoms. They can offer treatments that can ease symptoms, but it may be best to address one or two symptoms per visit.

You Are a Consumer

You are responsible for procuring comprehensive care, and your physicians can help. You are the central player of a team that seeks overall success; their job is to assist you with one part of that success. It may help you to think about your physicians as service providers and you are a consumer purchasing assistance for your condition. Drop your physicians if they refuse to cooperate, be understanding, or treat you as a team member in your own care. If you are having trouble finding the right providers and you need help it may be easier to consult the physician about individual symptoms. Name the symptom, state its severity (mild, moderate, severe), and request treatment for it.

If help is not forthcoming, if it's your physician's opinion that you will have to live with your condition as is, or if he or she thinks you are a psychiatric case, as a consumer you can shop around to find a cooperative physician. Do not allow embarrassment, guilt, or blame stop you from getting another opinion and another doctor.

Ensure Effective Office Visits

Communication problems are common during appointments, so it's important to communicate clearly with your doctor. Some tips on effective examining-room communication include the following.

- When you make the appointment, ask for some extra time to ask questions.

- If possible, set your appointments for first thing in the morning when your doctor will be on schedule and most likely will give you extra time.

- Prepare a complete list of your medications before each office visit, and include the dose you are actually taking.

- Keep notes on both positive and negative side effects from any newly prescribed medications.

- Prioritize the symptoms you wish to bring to the doctor's attention, and note their severity.

- If time is running out and you still have high-priority items on your agenda, schedule a follow-up visit right away to address these issues.

- Stay on track with your agenda. After the initial exchange of greetings, do not digress onto unrelated matters.

- Rehearse family members or friends who come with you to help you stay on track and avoid digressions.

- Be business-like in presenting your symptoms and succinct in answering your doctor's questions.

- Include depression and anxiety on your symptom list if they are present, but stay away from discussing your emotional distress. Most physicians view this as chitchat and expect you to go to a counselor for advice on such matters.

Explore Pain Management Clinics

Multidisciplinary pain clinics have provided some of the finest FM care on record. Professionals at such clinics include pain specialists, physical medicine and rehabilitation specialists, medical generalists, physical therapists, counselors, and social workers. However, pain management clinics that have only pain specialists, as valuable as that help is, cannot offer complete care.

Remember that painkillers are not the only medical treatment for FM and that medicine itself is not the only tool for managing FM. Complete care typically requires a full spectrum of adaptive training (as defined earlier in this chapter). You need physicians and other health-care providers for their expert contributions, including counselors for your emotional care.

Accept Your Limitations and Avoid Carelessness

Simple neglect may result in inadequate care or may counteract proper medical care. Forgetfulness about taking medications may be at fault for failure to control your symptoms. Purchase a pill organizer arranged by time of day and by day of the week to make sure you take your proper medications on time. Failure to go to bed at the same time each night and get regular sleep may be at the root of your poor awareness.

Problems are also brought on by indiscretions after you have made successful strides in your treatment. Overexertion can wipe away any progress you have made. Eventually, most people with FM learn how serious indiscretion is no matter what they do—cleaning the garage, camping in Montana, or playing softball with your children. Basic care requires an acceptance of your limitations.

Be Aware of Your Medical Coverage

It is distressing to see how many FM people are subject to the inverse law of health insurance coverage whereby the people who need health insurance the most are the least likely to get it. Individuals who apply for insurance and admit to fibromyalgia on the application are often rejected. Similarly, if FM leads to unemployment, it could mean loss of insurance benefits. Among those who do have benefits, some may have policies that require the insurance carrier's approval for consultants, specific services, or special diagnostic studies. If pain management is a denied benefit, or if the medications prescribed are not on the approved formulary, you have large gaps in coverage. As a backup, most states have a Medicaid program, but not everyone is eligible. As a result, individuals may fall through the cracks and end up with no medical coverage whatsoever.

Please note that consumer leverage in health maintenance organizations (HMOs) is nonexistent. These systems receive a fixed number of dollars per capita—a set dollar amount for each patient enrolled. In an HMO system, extra care for FM patients amounts to extra work but no extra profits. This system tends to make FM patients unwelcome.

You still might be able to find a helpful doctor in an HMO or other fixed-revenue system such as the Veterans Administration, but do not be surprised if you cannot. If FM is an unwelcome or unrecognized diagnosis, approach the doctor with specific symptoms, such as headaches, muscle aches, insomnia, and anxiety. Since medical treatment for FM proceeds by symptom, you can request treatment for symptoms without mentioning FM. Take extra time to seek out a different type of health insurance that will provide you with the medical treatment you need for dealing with your FM symptoms.

Control Your Stress

Stress management requires your rigorous attention, since stress aggravates your FM symptoms in direct proportion to the amount of your stress. If your living pattern is not compatible with FM, you will be in a constant battle with this illness. Stress is notorious for fueling pain, fatigue, and other FM symptoms and is generated wherever FM has disrupted your former lifestyle, from family and job roles to feelings of self-worth. Failure to manage the stresses of chronic illness means that your everyday life moves in a vicious downward spiral, and a crash is unavoidable. Many other illnesses are aggravated by stress, but FM is aggravated so predictably that proficiency in stress management is critical for adapting to FM.

Pain medication alone is inadequate to treat your symptoms. This fact was well documented in a study in the March–April 2002 issue of *Practical Pain Management*. In this study, chronic pain patients were tracked at three U.S. pain clinics before and after the September 2001 terrorist attacks. Pain was assessed on a scale of 0 to 10. The pain shot up from 4.1 (before the attacks) to 7.7 (after the attacks) and took months to settle down again. Medical treatment for pain was the only form of treatment noted at these clinics. Other studies showed that skills in stress management lessened the effects of stress after the terrorist attacks. Since stress is everywhere and causes chronic pain to flare, do not rely on painkillers alone for adequate treatment.

GET THE EMOTIONAL CARE YOU NEED

If FM is not a mental health problem, what can counselors offer? Most counselors deal with mental illness and because of the association of counseling with mental illness, FM people and families are quick to shun these professionals. Yet counselors have many services they can offer.

• Adaptive training for chronic illness: Since the emergence of HIV and AIDS, the number of counselors familiar with the emotional aspects of chronic illness has risen. Search one out; they have much they can teach you. More books on adaptation and adaptive training seminars are becoming available, so be sure to check the bookstore or library.

WHY PEOPLE WITH FIBROMYALGIA SHUN COUNSELING

When polling our support groups, we were not surprised to find inadequate emotional care since most people shy away from counseling, or therapy. It is a mistake to omit learning skills that apply to the emotional and social part of care. You and your family reduce your chances of achieving a satisfying lifestyle by not taking advantage of this type of support. At the very least, it stunts your potential growth and fulfillment.

Barely 10 percent of the FM people who answered our polls revealed that they have had more than a few sessions with a professional counselor. This is a critical inadequacy in the management of FM and goes a long way to explain the high failure rate in adapting. The 90 percent of support group members who did not receive counseling indicated that what specifically bothered them about seeing a counselor included fear of:

- Being viewed as crazy
- Being perceived as a hypochondriac
- The counselor discounting their pain
- Not being able to handle the stress
- Their spouse's thinking they are weak

Seeing a counselor does not mean you are mentally ill. You can see a counselor for help in dealing with a life-disrupting pain/fatigue illness, for assistance in adaptive training and handling setbacks, and for stress and crisis management. As with physicians, unknowledgeable counselors, such as a disability examiner, may discount FM as a diagnosis and view it as an imaginary condition or illegitimate illness. A competent counselor, however, will not view you as a hypochondriac and will help you adapt to FM. Fortunately, there are many excellent counselors who work with the emotional components of chronic illness. It is a matter of finding a knowledgeable counselor. We explore how to do that later in the chapter.

If you avoid counseling because you assume you already know enough about emotions, stress, and family systems, remember that few people handle stress well. Gaining every skill possible in handling stress can be helpful. If your fear is that your partner will view you as weak for seeking counseling, remember the extraordinary skills that are needed to adapt to FM. Your partner may also be afraid to see a counselor to work through his or her feelings as you both rebuild your lifestyles. Obtaining the help you need is imperative for your success, and it is immaterial who recognizes the need first. Without blame, the counselor can draw your spouse into therapy when the time is right.

• Help in dealing with blocks and traps: If you are struggling with blocks and traps refer to Chapter 7. A counselor can also help you.

• Stress/crisis management training: This Step Four task stabilizes your living pattern and prevents setbacks. Stress management can be learned from many sources, but counselors provide a readily available source.

Red Flags Signaling the Need for Counseling

Sadly, you and your family may wait until crisis has piled on top of crisis before seeking counseling. Of course, it is not a good idea to wait until desperation forces you to go to a counselor; but if that is the case be sure to find the help you need. If you identify with any of following red flags, you may benefit from talking to a professional counselor.

• Guilt

• Isolation

• Low sense of self-worth

• Frustration

• Lack of emotional support from your family

• Wishing you could live in the past

• Alienating yourself from friends and family

• Trying to please everyone

Finding a Counselor

Rapport with a counselor is important. Counselors should be licensed and fully qualified, and you and she or he need to have a connection in order to address your specific needs. You may want to schedule one session a week with a different counselor. At the end of a month, you can decide which one you will continue working with. If you make one appointment at a time, you should be prepared to move on if your rapport with a new counselor is weak. It may take more than one session to know if you found the right person, but make sure you find the right person to get as much support as you can.

Topics for Counseling

When you see a counselor, you may wish to simply say, "I have fibromyalgia—I'm here to learn to deal with it." Or you may go over a checklist of topics that typically come up in sessions with a counselor. You may want to try the topics we list here to coincide with the Four Steps to Adaptation.

In Step One, these topics are important to discuss:

- Coping with the life ordeal of chronic illness

- Completing grief work, including removing bitterness; reaching a composed acceptance of FM; and going beyond resignation to determination in managing FM

- Confronting and adapting to FM with your loved ones

- Recognizing and removing blocks that interfere with coping and adapting

- Managing setbacks and pitfalls

  In Step Two, these topics are important to discuss:

- Working with health-care providers

- Handling providers who discount you or accuse you of having an imaginary illness

  For Step Three, these topics are important to discuss:

- Redefining your self-worth and establishing means of making positive contributions

- Decision-making, overcoming the lethargy of FM, and taking action

- Reconstructing family roles that have been disrupted by FM

- Drawing your children into new constructive family roles

- Communicating, including the art of listening and defusing clashes

- Defining relationships with relatives, friends, and social circle

- Testing career aptitudes and starting job searches

  In Step Four, these topics are important to discuss:

- Stress/crisis management

- Relaxation techniques

Medical Insurance for Counseling

Insurance restrictions—which counselor you can see, how many visits you are allowed, how much is the copay, and so on—can present a problem. What if no competent counselors are available or you have no coverage for counselors? What if your insurance company limits you to six visits per year, and you've already gone for your six visits? After all, an investment of two or three years in counseling is realistic for dealing with a life-disrupting chronic illness. If insurance coverage is not available; we still recommend that you make a determined effort toward obtaining counseling. The following suggestions may help you get the counseling you need.

- Ask about a cash-pay plan to reimburse your counselor. While you may not be able to see the counselor weekly, you may be able to arrange some schedule, such as every two or three weeks.

- Consider state-funded agencies for people who have no insurance.

- Consider a pastoral counselor or religiously affiliated counseling center. Many of them are willing to provide counseling without charge or for a reduced fee.

- Ask your physician and support group for help in finding a counselor.

The tasks in Step Two required you to arm yourself with information and obtain the various types of treatment and support—particularly emotional support—that are necessary to build a fulfilling life. Now you can move forward to Step Three, the actual rebuilding process.

5

STEP THREE:
REBUILD YOUR LIFE AND
YOUR RELATIONSHIPS

◉

Congratulations on your arrival at Step Three! You have been working hard to improve your lifestyle, so take a minute to glance back to see how far you have come. How did you handle your illness before Step Two? How are you managing it now? Compare and congratulate yourself. Living may still be a struggle, but every challenge brings you new insight. You are honing old skills, gaining new ones, and learning everything you can about FM.

REBUILDING YOUR PATTERN OF LIVING
IN SIX DOMAINS

Progress at Step Two provides you with effective tools for Step Three, which is rebuilding a new pattern and way of life in what we call the Six Domains of Living. These six domains include:

- Self-worth

- Time and energy

- Family life

- Relationship with your spouse or partner

- Other relationships, including friends, relatives (outside your immediate family), your social circle

- Job or career

In this chapter, we will tackle each of these domains by providing feedback we gathered from other FM families. What has worked for them? What advice would you hear from an adaptive trainer or counselor? The suggestions are not fixed formulas that work for everyone, but offer some answers to your questions. The new lifestyle you build at Step Three will be your unique solution, made more attainable as you increase your knowledge and obtain new skills.

The tasks of rebuilding in the six domains of living can proceed arduously or smoothly. It depends on your vision and outlook of a rewarding future and your willingness to part with the past. If you are concerned about retaining who you have always been, if your sense of identity is tied to circumstances from the past then establishing a new reality will be more of a struggle until you can come to peace and let that old you go. Letting go of baggage from the past, focusing on finding a deeper sense of yourself, and claiming your new self as an FM person will make it easier to establish a new lifestyle.

DOMAIN ONE: REBUILDING YOUR SENSE OF SELF-WORTH

FM deeply influences your sense of self-worth, affecting different people in various ways. The following tips are some techniques you can use to improve your self-esteem.

1. Use your notes from Chapter 3 on the ways in which your sense of self-worth was affected to examine where you are at right now.
2. Ponder the meaning of self-worth. Do you know yourself? Do you have an innate sense of value and worth? Can you tap into this innate worth to positively boost your sense of self-worth?
3. After observing your current feeling of self-worth take a moment to review the losses you acquired as a result of your FM diagnosis.

As you read about conditions or issues that both can support self-worth and cause further setbacks, make note of the examples that pertain to you.

Issues Affecting Self-Worth

A number of issues affect your sense of self-worth. By defining and directly confronting them you can revitalize your sense of worthiness. As you consider your losses, ask yourself the following questions:

- Did my pursuits before having FM represent all life has to offer or are other things worthwhile?

- What other reasons are there for living? Are they different to those that carried me this far?

- What inner desires or motivations could I now utilize that I have never had time to incorporate into my life before?

- Am I really diminished by FM, or can I find another way of contributing to others in a new and deeper way?

- How can I take advantage of these changes and create a fulfilling lifestyle?

The key to rebuilding your sense of self-worth is to find your other strengths and build on them.

Lack of Finances or Loss of Career. One of the most common blows to a sense of self-worth is losing your ability to earn money. You may feel worthless if you have lost a job that once paid you a lot of money. To handle this situation, focus on your remaining personal strengths. If you see a counselor, he or she can guide you as you reexamine your skills and how you may use them in a different, yet still financially beneficial, way. While you do this, reassess your aptitudes and your job capacity to determine what you need to succeed in a new working environment. Refer to Appendix B for more information on how to assess your aptitudes and search for a new job or career opportunity.

Lack of Physical Activity. If you derive your sense of self from doing strenuous physical activities, you may now feel worthless as fibromyalgia has forced you to live a more sedentary lifestyle. Take it easy on yourself as you shift your focus from physical power to your underutilized mental and emotional aptitude and character strengths. Remember to ask yourself the questions previously discussed and focus on new areas in which to develop your strengths.

Lack of Social Life. If you are like some FM people, your identity is built on your flair for the social life. Try to look at these losses in physical and social activities as only external things. You have not lost your inner self; therefore, you do not need to depend so much on social interactions for your sense of self. Ask yourself, "Can I still be social, but in a different capacity?" Shift through your newly realized strengths and sense of worth discovered from the previous sections. "How do I use them to enhance my sense of social significance?"

Lack of Family Relations. Do you feel diminished in your reduced capacity for service-oriented family roles? Are you over-magnifying FM? Are you taking advantage of how medical care can help you recover some of your abilities? If the truth lies somewhere in the middle, then there are still things you can do to improve your ability to do some of these tasks. Explore the possibilities that may not have occurred to you before about how you can contribute to your family in ways that are not as physically demanding as your former roles.

Crisis of Faith. Many people who are dealing with a lifelong debilitating illness experience a crisis of faith where they feel destroyed by their illness. If you experience such a crisis, we can only tell you that FM is not a message from heaven or a punishment from God. Ask yourself what is your view of a supreme being and whether it is influenced by emotional turmoil of the past. Counseling, pastoral or otherwise, may help you to reestablish your sense of worth in the face of such a crisis. You may find as you gain more intimate knowledge into your inner self that you are building a stronger relationship with your higher power.

With a significantly changed career or work life and reduction in your roles at home, you face some staggering losses. In facing your losses, ask yourself these questions:

- Is my life still something precious, or is it an unending ordeal of compromise and endurance?

- What does it mean to be worthwhile to myself and to others?

- In what ways do I still have any power to accomplish things that are helpful to me and others?

- Despite the limitations of FM, can I still have a life that is worth living?

Your answers to these questions may have surprised you. There are more opportunities than you previously thought. You are approaching your situation with a new perspective that will open up new horizons and that may lead you to an equally or even more fulfilling way of life.

Internal, Interpersonal, and External Adjustments

When working to build a sense of worth, it may help to divide your work into tasks that strengthen your internal, or innate, sense of worth; your sense of worth derived from relationships; and the external supports to self-worth.

Internal Sense of Self-Worth. One approach to strengthening your innate sense of worth is to ask yourself these questions:

- Who am I?

- What part of my identity is based in my childhood or past experiences?

- Do I need other people or responsibilities in my life to make me feel good about myself?

- Have I handled personal challenges in the past where I surprised myself with my own self-sufficiency?

Once you answer these questions take some time with a counselor or other trusted member of your support network to discuss your discoveries.

Methods to Heighten Self-Worth

Desensitization is an approach to ease a wounded sense of self-worth that is performed with a therapist. In the counseling sessions, bring up the negative barbs that have slowly negated your sense of self over the years. You and your counselor will be able to systematically neutralize these barbs so they lose their sharpness.

For example, the therapist may turn down the lights in the room and ask you to imagine that you are sitting at the back of a movie theater watching an emotionally traumatic scene from earlier in your life. The therapist asks you to watch only a small section of the scene at a time. This part may cause a strong response to burst forth. Your counselor will work through this reaction with you so you have an adult understanding of what happened. In future visits, the therapist may bring you back to this place to observe from other angles, and the same scene will not arouse such harsh emotions. Eventually you will be able to closely examine this and other previously painful experiences without reacting. In this way, you become less sensitive to the sharpness of the barbs from previous life experiences, and you can apply what you have learned to other areas of your life.

Using positive affirmations can also help you strengthen your sense of worth. We all remember the bad things and often beat ourselves up by repeating negative thoughts to ourselves. "I'm so stupid." "I can't do anything right." Positive affirmations are beneficial statements that you say to yourself about how you want to be or feel. "I am smart." "I can do this right." Many people think that if you say something enough you start to believe it; so stop repeating the negative stuff and start validating the good things about yourself and your life.

Meditation, or prayer, is another technique to explore. Innumerable people with FM attest to the power of meditation and prayer for self-renewal. While meditating or praying, align yourself with a higher presence and put the primacy of yourself aside. In psychological terms, the conflicting demands of your physical self become muted or surrendered, resulting in a sense of renewal. There are so many resources available on meditation and prayer; and there is no right or wrong way. You can try to keep all thoughts out of your mind, internally recite certain prayers, or even use positive affirmations to reenergize and refocus.

Sense of Worth from Healthy Relationships and Strong Family Membership.
Membership in a good family can boost your sense of worth. A close-knit family that is accepting even in illness can be a very positive influence on your sense of self. Your main concern may be whether your family or spouse cherishes you as much now as before you had FM, for the committed support of your partner forms a pillar for your sense of self-worth.

However, the opposite may apply to your casual friends whose opinions may not form a reliable base for your self-worth. In your social circles, you may encounter various kinds of intolerance. Your primary concern in this arena is to protect yourself from stigma, doubt, and discrimination. Are you able to override someone else's negative opinion of you? Are you assured that your innate self is fully worthy despite the unkind acts or remarks of others? The ability to rise above the judgments of social friends, or even strangers, is liberating, since other people's vacillating opinions can make your emotional life a roller coaster. Concentrate on your internal sense of value to free yourself from a constant source of turmoil.

External Worth. Tangible external supports may be the easiest area of self-worth to handle. You manage these supports in a mechanical sense by arranging for chores to get done, setting up your social calendar, and engineering your job or career so that it fits your needs. Still, it may be difficult to maintain, but be sure to continually review your options, make plans, schedule events, and work in a way that you feel like an active participant in her life and the world. Having things to do, to think about, and be a part of makes us feel needed and worthy.

DOMAIN TWO: REBUILDING YOUR TIME AND ENERGY

Your resources of time and energy are hit hard by chronic illness. To have fibromyalgia means that your energy is always in short supply. And to be constantly drained by chronic illness has an additional effect—it bends your sense of time. You may be constantly aware of being behind schedule, of taking longer to do things, of forever chasing time, and of wasting more time than you use. While you may be aware of the value of gauging and pacing your energy, you may not realize the shrewdness required to handle time. In *Good Days, Bad Days: The Self in Chronic Illness and Time*, sociologist Kathy Charmaz notes that when chronic illness bends time, it creates what she calls *temporal incongruence*—the distortion of time perspectives and the ability to plan. Researchers report that clumsy time management interferes with every effort to achieve quality living. It interferes with:

- Maintaining the supports to your sense of self-worth

- Procuring the complete care for your health needs

- Coordinating action designed to bring fulfillment in your life

The hardest thing about distorted time is that your ability to plan is weakened, which may force you to live one day at a time. You are mired in today's struggles, such as bathing, dressing, taking your medications on schedule, preparing your food, and doing necessary housework. Your vision of time encompasses only your tasks of today, not the challenges you will face in future months or years. Living one day at a time fails to take into account the big picture and your goals of a fulfilling lifestyle. Instead, you suffer losses in terms of self-supports, the future, prestige and accomplishment, security, hopes, dreams, and plans. Living one day at a time feeds into a sense of hopelessness, social isolation, and the helpless victim state. For these reasons, it is imperative that you learn proficiency in time management. To do so compensates for the ravages of temporal incongruence.

Effective Time Management

You can gain skills in time management from a number of sources. For example, you can study it in such books as *Time Management from the Inside Out* by Julie Morgenstern. You may also wish to attend seminars or purchase videotapes on time management.

Take advantage of daily planner books. These calendar-books are far more than aids for the absent-minded. A planner is a tool for daily use that helps straighten out the bent-time distortion. Keep in mind that planner books should never be used to force yourself to do more than fatigue allows. They are best used as a spreadsheet to position your time and energy to best meet your priorities and most meaningful goals.

Purchase a book with ample space (some come with carrying straps). You want room for handy lists, memos to yourself, and for jotting down what you might forget. Most of all, you want to be able to view an entire month in one glance. You can plot your future on this spreadsheet. You can arrange and rearrange your schedule, and later you can review your maneuvers and learn from your mistakes. The following are pointers for working in your planner:

• Balance: Mark down tasks that contribute to your long-range goals as well as the urgent necessities of daily living.

PATTI'S SAMPLE TIME PLANNER

Long-Range Goals

- Do not overextend myself.
- Build a regular schedule that is easy to remember.

Prime time: Afternoons (Try to keep Tuesdays and Wednesdays as the main day for priority appointments that occur every month at the same time.) Book all priority appointments three to six months in advance. Take advantage of long-term commitments that do not change—always at same time of day.

- Water exercise therapy—Every Tues. 2:00 P.M.
- Pain management—1st Wed. 2:00 P.M. every month
- Therapist—2nd Wed. 2:00 P.M. every month
- Support group—3rd Wed. 6:30–8:30 P.M. every month
- Nail appoint—3rd Thurs. 2:00 P.M. every month—(If I have energy)
- Thursday lightest day

Out-and-About Days: Make a list of one errand to do after each appointment on Wednesday to save unnecessary car trips. Since leaving the house costs two hours in travel and preparation time, make the most of each outing. After every Wed. appointment:

- Go grocery shopping
- Pick up/drop off dry cleaning
- Purchase needed office supplies
- Pick up prescriptions dropped off previous Wed.

Coordinate dog grooming appointments with Tuesdays or Fridays when I plan to put clean sheets on my bed!

Allow for Proper Rest Time and Planning:

- Keep Mondays open to plan the rest of the week, make to-do lists and organize; perfect time to wash hair, do laundry.
- Try to stay home either on Monday or Friday of each week.
- Reserve Saturdays to sleep in and go out to dinner to relax.
- Keep Sundays as family days to enjoy.

- Prime time: Schedule your most demanding tasks around your expected peak productivity times.

- Prioritize: Mark low-priority and frivolous items as "optional" or "if I still have energy."

- Quality time: Plan playful diversions that fulfill you.

- Out-and-about days: Cluster your errands so that your automobile time is used efficiently. Since it takes effort to prepare, consider doing more than one errand at a time.

- Density of entries: Be realistic! Don't cram too much into your schedule. Allow yourself enough time for proper rest and make sure your scheduled items are truly achievable. If not, spread them out. As long as you provide for your long-term goals on a regular basis, progress is inevitable.

Energy Planning

People without FM may have energy to burn and can get away with paying little attention to their bodily needs and energy levels. As an FM sufferer, you have no such luxury. To achieve results, you must balance your energy as an accountant would balance money. After plotting and scheduling time in your planner, look at the following pointers for reevaluating your energy expenditures.

- Time of day patterns: Mark down your best hours of the day as well as the times you might need rest or restful activity.

- Energy costs: Differentiate between high-energy and low-energy tasks in your planner and how much rest and recovery is required for each one. For example, one unit of energy might mean the amount of energy expended in an hour when you feel reasonably well.

  Low-energy activities: watching TV, telephone calls, paying bills

  Medium-energy activities: vacuuming, laundry, cleaning

  High-energy activities: leaving house for any reason

Patti's Sample Energy Allotment Planner

Time of Day Patterns

- *Hardest time of day 7:00 A.M. to 10:00 A.M.:* Waiting for pain medications to kick in and morning soreness/discomfort to ease up so cannot start preparing to leave house until around noon. Out the door at 12:30 to 1:00 P.M.
- *Best time of day 12:00 P.M. to 4:00 P.M.:* Do most important on-the-road activities.
- *Return home and crash:* Lie down between 4:30 P.M. and 6:00 P.M. to recoup.
- *Somewhat recharged by 7:00 P.M.:* Serve dinner, clean kitchen, and feed dogs.
- *Sit in recliner from 9:30 P.M. to 11:30 P.M.:* Read newspapers, make lists, try to find misplaced things I'll need tomorrow (chair time makes movement possible).
- Work on computer or finish up chores from 12:00 P.M. to 1:00 A.M. (Often takes until 3:00 A.M. to unwind enough to sleep again.)

- Energy planning: Notice what tasks you reserve for peak energy times.

- Analyze your estimates: In your planner, check the accuracy of your time estimates; this allows you to more easily schedule in the future.

Working with a Counselor

With fibromyalgia, your physical energy is limited, but mental fatigue also imposes limits on your accomplishments. Even with the best planning you might fail to attain your goals because of mental indecision. Your intentions may not result in action. This form of fatigue with its lack of purposeful activity is prevalent in both FM and chronic fatigue syndrome, and should be discussed with a counselor.

There are many types of counseling or therapy. Cognitive behavioral techniques, more than other forms of counseling, produce goal-oriented and concrete action. Not every person who wants to find a cognitive behavioral therapist will locate someone with that exact title. Nevertheless, most counselors use behavioral techniques in one form or another. The terms *behavioral therapy, reality therapy, rational emotive behavioral therapy,* and *cognitive behavioral therapy* may all be used. Most counselors assemble their approaches to include these techniques.

A behavioral therapist will ask you what your goals are and how you are going to accomplish them. He or she will want to know how you want your daily living patterns to change, what obstacles stand in your way, and (when these obstacles are removed), how you would then proceed to reach your goals. The counselor thus helps you specify your goals and the obstacles in your way, while you mentally rehearse tactics and formulate plans. When an acceptable plan emerges, you commit to carrying it out. Your actions are later reviewed and assessed for effectiveness. Refinements are devised to improve your effectiveness in the future. You may wonder whether this technique is effective, and we found information while working on the book that shows using cognitive behavioral therapy can be invaluable.

Behavioral therapy usually can be completed relatively quickly if your goals are limited; perhaps in two or three months. As soon as your goals are identified, the counselor serves as your consultant on them. The first sessions will be dedicated to establishing action goals. The counselor will ask:

- What things do you need to accomplish?

- What short-term and long-term goals are most important to you?

- In what ways do you want this week to proceed differently from last week?

This process will eliminate vague, impractical goals, such as "getting my life back" or "being involved with my family." Instead, you will narrow down specific, concrete goals, such as "to go out once a week with my family for a recreational activity"; "to find a job that is easier on my health"; or "to get out of the house twenty hours per week to do volunteer work."

Next, the counselor will ask you what is holding you back from accomplishing these goals so that obstacles can be identified. Again, it is the specifics that concern the behavioral therapist. Some obstacles may include the fears of failing and feeling devastated, looking foolish, and not being able to complete your goal.

At this point, your sessions may involve examining the errors and misperceptions that often interfere with constructive action. For example, the therapist might examine how fear of failing constitutes the error of catastrophizing (where you over-imagine the worst); most likely your assumption that failure is inevitable is overdone. Another error is over-generalizing, or assuming that one experience forebodes a generally bad outcome in broader settings.

Finally, the therapist works with you to accomplish your goals. If you have had a pattern of housebound immobility, for example, a behavioral approach would call for you to begin with preliminary actions, such as driving to the shopping mall three times per week, checking prices on at least two items, and returning home. While this is not a finished goal, it gets you out of the house and breaks the spell of immobility. From this beginning, it becomes much easier for you to step up to the goals that you initially stated.

SALLY'S STORY: USING A COUNSELOR TO SET AND ACCOMPLISH GOALS

Sally, a woman with FM, lived with her two adult children. Her level of functioning was low; she did a few house chores and accomplished little outside the home except for a daily walk around the block. For transportation, she depended on her children but felt reticent to impose on them. She had served in the military overseas, had suffered posttraumatic stress in civil riots, and had a counselor at a Veterans Administration (VA) clinic. She once saw a physician outside the VA who concurred with the diagnosis of posttraumatic stress disorder (PTSD) but made an additional diagnosis of FM. However, at the VA clinic her treatment was limited to PTSD, and she had no medical coverage outside the VA.

The counselor at the VA decided on a behavioral approach. The client's immediate goals were discussed and identified as these:

- To enroll in the state Medicaid program to receive insurance for health care outside the VA
- To find local health-care givers
- To regularly go to office visits and upgrade the quality of her health care
- To improve her health in this manner sufficiently so that she would be able to drive safely by herself

A troublesome obstacle was Sally's hesitance to impose on her family for transportation. They had very busy lives as young working adults. Her concerns were explored at length with the counselor. The family's system of delegating roles was examined, and an exchange system for home chores was devised so that Sally felt comfortable asking her children for rides.

Sally's shame over needing public assistance, Medicaid, was also addressed. She agreed to go on brief information-gathering trips to the Medicaid office. A couple of employees there were rude, which became another obstacle, but this was also addressed. Sally then made plans for obtaining Medicaid and was successful in procuring it. She had not yet confronted her fear of failing the test for a driver's license. She had driven well before, and it required little practice for her to regain confidence behind the wheel. Again, her near-phobic fears of dealing with a public agency came up. The counselor and Sally agreed that she would make exploratory trips to the agency to become familiar with the layout, the waiting time, and the procedures. This gave her feedback on her fears of the agency and allowed her to face and resolve them. Subsequently her application for a driver's license was successful. Sally was then able to drive herself to medical appointments.

DOMAIN THREE: REBUILDING YOUR FAMILY LIFE

How much comfort do you receive from your immediate family—those who live under the same roof with you? Is your family a haven for you, a refuge from the discords in the world? If one member of your family experiences a setback, such as a chronic illness, do all of the other members rally to bring assistance? As a haven and rallying point, your family can be a potent resource in the face of adversity. Unfortunately, in our day, the strengths of the family are seldom well developed and the family's system of operation may quickly shut down in the face of a challenge like FM. In this section, we look at how a family gets sent off balance and how its operational strengths can be restored.

Disrupting the Delicate Balance

Is your family resilient? Can it deploy its resources and modify its roles if a member becomes ill? FM can disrupt almost all family activities, including eating meals together, going on outings, doing recreational activities, expressing encouragement to each other and loyalty to the family, doing chores and taking responsibility for getting tasks done, and giving and receiving affection and respect. Parents are rarely trained in family dynamics nor are they well prepared for marriage and family. The added strain of illness can destabilize the family structure enough that often it crumbles. In this sense, we use the term "family" to refer to the most important people in your life, the ones who are around most often or who you are responsible for.

However, reconstruction is quite possible with the help of family therapists who are experts in family dynamics. Family therapists and psychologists can reestablish a healthy balance of interactions, and your family can benefit from these specialized services. If you value your family, you will want this kind of assistance.

Setting Up Communication and Rearranging Roles

Communication in your family can be improved, but it requires the willingness of all parties involved. This task includes practice in the art of listening to each other, acknowledging each other's perspectives, and asking each other for elaboration and clarification of views. Another part is learning to express personal feelings to other family members without insinuation, blame, or accusation. These communication skills can be practiced and learned.

After working on improving communication, you need to restructure the roles of your family members so that the needs of your illness are dealt with, but also so it's not overwhelming for each member. Remember, people have a range of abilities—not all can take on the same amount. You can brainstorm the situation using the following questions.

- What do you (the FM sufferer) need for both physical and emotional support?

- What can your family members do to help you achieve these needs?

- What are you still able to do or want to be involved with in your family?

- What modifications in your usual activities are necessary so you can more actively participate in all activities? (For example, maybe you can participate in card games when you cannot go to the park.) Every family needs to be creative in finding these solutions.

- What new and constructive ways can you add to your family's lifestyle? Turn these contributions into definite, expected roles.

- What can your family do to respect your roles so you still feel the responsibility and control in how you do them as before?

A common but well-meaning error is when family members try to do everything so that you do not have to lift a finger. This deprives you of opportunities to be helpful and constructive to the family. Without such roles, you may begin to feel helpless, dependent, and incapable of doing anything worthwhile, which leads to other FM symptoms and possibly depression.

Instead, the family should search for things you can do while sparing you from tasks that exceed your capacity. For example, you may be able to plan meals and cook but not unload the groceries from the car. You may be able to do many tasks in rearing, comforting, and caring for your children, and you can arrange the family's social and recreational activities. A well-coordinated, communicating family makes sure that you have a variety of areas in which you can contribute but also that you have assistance when approaching the limit of your capacity. You and your family will need to be more vocal as you work out each member's needs and roles and how they feel about the changes.

Negotiating Roles

The meaning of family and marriage has changed in recent decades as families are not as closely knit as they used to be. We live in a do-your-own-thing culture, where the home serves simply as a place for sleeping and eating for family members who lead independent lives. This shift toward autonomy can make relating more difficult as family members shrug off the need for emotional closeness.

How do you handle these difficulties in your own family? Members of your family may not feel inclined to cooperate with each other, preferring instead to base their relationships on an exchange of favors. Ultimately, you may find yourself facing FM and fending for yourself unless you assert yourself and ask for assistance. To handle this difficulty, you need your contribution to be recognized and to negotiate what you are entitled to in return. Many observers of today's society regard arrangements such as these as a breakdown of traditional family values. The situation may be regrettable; but if this is your family's operational basis, then you need to negotiate to obtain assistance from each family member.

Discussing Fibromyalgia with Children

Another issue that comes up in rebuilding your immediate family relationships is how to discuss fibromyalgia with your children. Children, especially young ones, need to know what this illness is doing to you, their FM-affected mother or father. They need to know simply, directly, and honestly. Children need to be reassured that while you are ill, you will survive and will continue to be with them and love them. Once communication in your family becomes operational, children can also be drawn into the circle of mutual listening and expressing. They, too, can help in the family adjustments that are needed for you to function.

We highly recommend family conferences, and a family therapist can do wonders in setting the tone for these conferences, which can then be carried on without the therapist. Generally, the tone of the conference should be simple enough for children to understand what is being discussed and to offer their comments. Children's views should be respected, yet parental roles for guiding and nurturing should not be set aside. The following pointers will help you set up and run family meetings.

- Designate one member as the initiator to call the meeting each week.

- Everyone should have the opportunity and be expected to speak without interruption.

- After a family member speaks, ask for elaboration and clarification of statements made by the speaker before moving to the next person.

- Discuss, validate, and resolve issues brought up by each member.

- Discuss and resolve emotional turmoil.

- Discuss and resolve practical matters, such as transportation and chores.

- Check to make sure that you are all working together, and that each member feels part of the team. Often the weekly meeting is the family's primary means of connecting. If your connectedness has waned during the intervening week, the meeting is the time to reestablish it.

Family Life with Juvenile Fibromyalgia

Unfortunately, the medical reality is that juveniles can develop fibromyalgia. Remission in young people is more likely than in adults—and possibly more likely in boys than in girls—but the majority of juveniles with FM can expect major life disruptions. In any community, you may find physicians who brush off FM as "growing pains" and others who recognize the diagnosis. To find the right doctor, you will need persistence.

The next hurdle is the battle within your family to accept the reality of your child's illness. This battle is fought in layers. The first layer might be to determine whether any faking is taking place. After that, the question becomes whether any changes should be made because of FM. Not just parents, but every member of your family fights the battle for acceptance. Siblings need to learn that your family's complexion has changed and that they will need to relate to a new reality. You, as a parent, may be agonized with guilt and feelings like failure. Then the wonderful day arrives when your whole family, parents and siblings, all recognize FM in your family member, treating this person with respect and handling the FM as an established routine.

The remaining hurdles are in the school and social worlds. Children with FM are suddenly different from their peers, no longer capable of winning peer membership or distinction on a level playing field. A child with an invisible illness may find no mercy with peers or with the school authorities and be asked, "Are you really ill? Isn't this an excuse to slough off? You've always done fine, so what is your real story?" A firmly worded letter from your doctor to the school authorities may excuse your child from strenuous activities. Perhaps the need for home instruction will become apparent. But sometimes nothing happens. Most social and school environments need to be solidly convinced before they will accommodate FM children, and convincing them can be a struggle. Society can be cruel to children with chronic illness, and you, as parent, need to take action.

• Guard your child's self-esteem. Your child's self-esteem is already under threat since illness makes him or her different from other children. Yet if you fully trust your child and believe her about her symptoms, you protect her self-esteem. If you encourage her endeavors and validate her efforts, even if they do not meet the standards of her energetic peers, she will not feel handicapped. Doing this requires extra time, patience, and effort on your part.

• Become an advocate for your child's educational and medical needs. Some pediatricians might brush off FM as "growing pains." Schools may overrule your requests for home schooling and not respect your child's right to accommodation. In dealing with these situations, you need to be as proactive on behalf of your child as you would be for your spouse or yourself—and depending on how you take care of yourself, maybe even more so. Try looking for information at the website pediatricnetwork.org or in the book *Wrightslaw: From Emotions to Advocacy* by Pamela Wright and Peter Wright.

• Compensate for social and cultural deprivations your child may experience. Television is no substitute for live performances such as a school play, going on field trips, or meeting people from different parts of the world. You will have to work harder to get your child to social events and to his or her friends' houses—and for those friends to come over to your house. In addition, the Internet may offer a special social world when your child finds Internet pen pals who have similar illnesses.

Understanding and communication are necessities throughout the transition from adolescence to adulthood for any youngster. The transition is all the more needed when your child has juvenile FM. The usual struggles may take on greater intensity. But youth must arrive at their own conclusions—no amount of parental advice can completely shield them from the struggle. We offer the following tips if you have a child or children struggling with FM.

• Review the ideas for support people in the Four Steps to Adaptation system as they apply to you as parent. The Step One struggles of support people are those that you, as parent, have to deal with. The sooner you can fully acknowledge the reality of your child's illness, the sooner you can put realistic plans for dealing with it into action. Responsibility for your child's overall care (Step Two) falls to you.

• Since parental roles are greatly expanded, you can quickly be overwhelmed and suffer caregiver exhaustion. Parents need respites; two parents can alternate in carrying out caregiving responsibilities. Parents also need time together to renew their relationship with each other. They need help from all sources in the family. See the discussion in Chapter 7 for more information on relieving caregiver exhaustion.

• Learn to talk to your child about chronic illness. You may wish to insulate yourself from the reality of your child's illness by not talking about it. But the illness is real, and you need to acknowledge it fully. To give your child the support, encouragement, and validation he needs, you cannot turn your back on him because he has a chronic illness.

• Recruit professional assistance from child psychologists and family therapists. Seek out professionals in child psychology to see how your child is behaving in these new circumstances. These specialists can work with you to help your child accept and adapt to how they are now different than they used to be and how they are different from other kids. You may also explore what your child needs to have a fulfilling childhood despite FM.

DOMAIN FOUR: REBUILDING YOUR RELATIONSHIP WITH YOUR PARTNER

FM takes its toll on marriage. When emotionally charged matters surface in your marriage, it's important to get professional help promptly. The best time to take action is the minute your relationship gets choppy. A counselor helps protect your marriage by showing you and your partner how to focus on your friendship with each other, rather than letting fibromyalgia come between the two of you. Your relationship will probably go through a sequence of changes in adapting to FM. Both you and your partner initially may defy the illness and the reality of FM. Then, as you both start to accept the reality of FM, you set up caregiving and care-receiving roles. Finally, these roles are refined and your relationship begins to function on a new level that makes accommodation for FM. Refer to Chapter 9 for more information on rebuilding your life with your partner.

DOMAIN FIVE: REBUILDING RELATIONSHIPS WITHIN YOUR SOCIAL CIRCLE—FRIENDS AND RELATIVES

The difficult domain of rebuilding relationships with your relatives outside your immediate family as well as your friends calls for serious attention because they may react in surprising ways to your chronic illness. Consult a therapist to talk through the feelings that the new interactions with these friends and relatives bring up in you.

Rejection from Friends

Rejection is when people pretend to accept your condition but follow that acceptance with intolerance and rejection. These people at first seem sympathetic but then treat you as though you were making up the illness. They believe that you are able to carry on perfectly well, and consequently, they become upset when you are

MANAGING PAIN WITH THE STIGMA OF FIBROMYALGIA

People with chronic illness are often stigmatized in both social and health-care settings. Many FM sufferers avoid hospitals and doctors, hiding their pain because of the misunderstandings and stigmas attached to medication. Norma, a registered nurse (RN) with FM, provides invaluable advice for those dealing with FM pain and the harsh stigma that is attached to taking pain medications. Having worked as a hospital nurse for over twenty years, she has firsthand experience with the stigma of chronic illness in her social circle and in a health-care setting. Here is what she had to say:

To ignore an FM patient's orders for pain medication is, of course, deplorable. Fortunately, most nurses are conscientious, and for them to ignore a patient is the exception and not the rule. But unfortunately, during a hospital stay of several days, a large number of nurses and staff members might rotate on and off a given case. Now and then you encounter a nurse who undermedicates. The problem is a real one. The 0 to 10 pain-rating scale has helped the problem, since the scale is used in all hospitals. This scale alerts caregivers of the presence of pain. But despite the scale, an FM person might be mistaken for a drug seeker, crank, or incessant complainer.

FM patients resemble drug seekers because their need for medication is higher than what most patients need—already one red flag. Another red flag goes up if the patient requests medication sooner than the schedule calls for it. Further doubts might arise due to the opinions of the nurse, who might think that FM is a hokey illness. So here is a patient with a supposed phony illness wanting high doses of pain medicine and calling for it sooner than it is scheduled. Let's assume there is no history of drug abuse in the past. Administering pain medication should be routine, like giving insulin to diabetics. Generally this is what does happen, but misjudgments can occur. Society has bent views of FM, and these views can influence caregivers. Then people needing medication might not get it. However, hospitals always have an in-house nursing supervisor around the clock. They are troubleshooters. Simply call the hospital operator and ask for the nursing supervisor for the hospital, and you will receive help.

In addition, the 0 to 10 system can sometimes fail. For example, suppose the patient says the pain level is 6, and the orders say to give plain Tylenol for 6 or less? This patient may have strong intravenous medication waiting to be used if the pain is 7 or more. I've seen people crying in pain, and when asked about it they report 6 and get plain Tylenol. So the scale is imprecise, and if the patient minimizes on the assessment she may get inadequate treatment.

CONTINUED

If you have medication on order and are reporting your pain level correctly, but you still find the medicine is not strong enough, you must take this problem up with your doctor. Tell your doctor what your requirements for pain medication have been in the past. That serves as a guide to the amount of medication now needed in the hospital. Also, you can ask your doctor about an infusion pump, sometimes called PCA [patient-controlled anesthesia]. This pump has a bedside button that allows you some control over the medication without calling a nurse. Another way to get the medication adjusted is for the nurse to page the physician and report that the pain is not adequately controlled. The order can then be changed.

If you need to be admitted into the hospital, be sure you are admitted under your primary care doctor. You can arrange for your primary care doctor to admit or to consult as long as the doctor is on staff at the hospital you will go to. When your own doctor admits or consults, you have an advocate who is already familiar with your needs and your case.

not able to maintain the same social pace. Even if you remind them of what you have already told them about your illness, the ostracism process has already begun.

Should you confront these people? To do so turns into a crusade for your right to exist with illness. Instead, stick to your mission of bringing fulfillment to your life. Don't spend time or energy on unsatisfying relationships. If you know a friend is going to disrespect you and discussion gets you nowhere, then it is in your best interest to dissociate yourself from this person and let her or him go.

Strategies for Coping with Negative Reactions to Fibromyalgia

In interacting with friends and acquaintances, you are not totally at their mercy. You have options—total nondisclosure, controlled disclosure, and full disclosure— in how you present yourself. The pros and cons of each approach are discussed in the following paragraphs.

Total Nondisclosure. The threat of being discredited—the menace of stigma— may deter you from disclosing your health status. Nondisclosure is a prime option since FM is invisible to most observers. In using this option, you are simply careful about your self-presentation so that you betray little about your limitations. Few people will guess, and you certainly are not required to make announcements. After all, some things are private—your bank account, your sex life, and your health status. You can retain social contacts and enjoy them on a simple level as these are not people who know you well. In addition, if disclosure can be used against you, it may be in your best interest to choose your confidants with care. When a friend asks you how you are doing, you do not have to treat it as a request for a report on your health. Your answer can be as simple as, "Fine, and how are you?"

If you want to discuss FM, however, you should feel no shame, but proceed cautiously on your terms. It may be hard to hold yourself back and just talk about polite topics when FM is the central struggle of your life. But in most social settings, you reap momentary pity and no lasting compassion.

So where can you safely talk about FM and find support? You can do it with close family and true friends, at your support group, and with your counselor.

Controlled Disclosure. Controlled disclosure means that you give a regulated, limited presentation of your health status. Maybe you would prefer not to disclose your situation at all, but sometimes circumstances make it necessary for your safety. With certain friends, relatives, or associates you can normalize the illness so it's not a hot topic for you. Your manner and bearing will convey that you are not a sympathy seeker; you are in control and you are informed about FM or the part of the illness you present. Since FM is a common illness, people may come to you with questions while others may want your views and support.

Controlled disclosure is often used in a work setting in which nondisclosure is not possible. You moderate the information that you give out about you and FM. You make it clear to your coworkers and your supervisor that you can still perform your duties by pacing yourself and that your abilities and commitment have not changed. This level of disclosure offers you partial protection against stigmas and prejudicial reactions that could arise were you to remain silent. For example, if your work associates put on a dinner party, to be sociable you present yourself as a relatively healthy person and decide how much they see of your illness. Perhaps you save up your energy and participate as if you don't have FM, or you find a chair and sit with your friend or spouse. Although your associates know of your illness, your appearance enables you to interact like an unaffected person.

You may also find yourself modifying disclosure in your family circles. At a gathering of relatives, for example, you may sense that some people now feel uneasy around you and may understate your symptoms and carry on as though you were feeling quite well.

As a maneuver, controlled disclosure has limitations. Your best efforts rarely normalize your social presentation completely, and your friends may demand a lot of energy from you despite your request for low-energy activities. Make sure you have explained the illness, your limitations, and your wish to continue your association with them on this basis—that is all you can do. If they do not respect your needs it is time to end the relationship. Do not beat yourself up because you are not at fault.

Full Disclosure. This third option should be reserved for quality friends—the people you are the closest to. When you reveal to these friends that you have FM for the first time, you might not know in advance how they will react. Some may react with discomfort, stigma formation, or rejection. Nevertheless, if you wish to retain these people as lifelong friends, you need to divulge that you have FM and that it imposes limitations. True friends accept you and work through their reactions to these new circumstances both with you and on their own. With them, you can fully disclose about your life with FM; you feel comfortable and validated to talk about FM or anything else. These friends value communication and socializing over activity. These friends are usually flexible; for example, if it is a day when your symptoms are acting up, you can change your plans and do something inactive, or you can cancel without worrying about their reaction. Time together is important, not mileage traversed, places visited, and tangible objectives accomplished.

Disclosing that you have FM purges your social circle. Fair-weather friends can be replaced. If your relationship was superficial, the loss will probably not be great. Fortunately, it is possible to cultivate a new circle of friends, either on your own or with your spouse and family. The great thing about friends is that you can make them at any time in your life.

Rebuilding Relationships with Relatives

While intolerant friends can be replaced, your relatives continue to be related to you regardless of their social attitudes. Here, "relatives" refers to extended family members, not to your immediate household. Desertions and losses among relatives—people you expect to be loyal and supportive—can be very disappointing.

Just when you need a lot of support, the closeness you have had with some relatives may dissipate. As you become ill, they may distance themselves from you. They may be unaware of their inner processes and insist that nothing has occurred to cut them off from you.

Generally, counselors urge caution about breaking off with relatives, more so than with social friends. If you have an angry falling-out with a relative, it may cut you off from that person for the rest of your life. This relative might be lacking in courtesy and reason, conflict may be inevitable, and the distancing may be even desirable. But most counselors recommend doing everything in your power to keep the channels of communication open. This can require delicate skill! These stress-provoking people, in denying that you have a legitimate problem and in pushing their bad advice at you, can cause you heartache and worsen FM symptoms. Try not to take them seriously. Keep a balanced outlook and remain respectful without letting them get to you. In time, your side of the issue and the reality of your condition may eventually be appreciated. In the meantime, however, you have maintained your connectedness with this part of the family.

What if there is no hope that this relative will come around? One thing to consider is whether you had had a meaningful relationship with this person prior to the onset of FM. Consider whether this is a continuation of a relationship or a recent change in attitude and behavior toward you. If there was no meaningful connection pre-FM, it may now be more difficult than ever to build at this time. To spend a lot of time and energy on this relationship will cause you to suffer, so do what you can to feel good about your part.

DOMAIN 6: REBUILDING YOUR JOB OR CAREER

As discussed earlier, maneuvering in the job world can be extremely difficult when you are trying to deal with the challenges of fibromyalgia.

Assessing Your Options

You may handle your work situation in any number of ways after the onset of FM. These may include the following:

- Stopping work altogether by retiring or taking permanent leave with or without disability benefits

- Reducing your hours or workload by easing job demands

- Shifting careers and changing to a job environment that better accommodates your health

For those who have to work, the third option may have more potential than fighting an ongoing battle with a tough job or career. Yet it is an option that is used less often and sometimes avoided with excuses ranging from the belligerent "I can't change jobs!" to the dramatic "This is my life! I'd sooner die than throw in the towel on my career." You may have a prized career or job, but close investigation is called for if the job compromises your quality of life. In our society, the work ethic is strong, but you have to make your health needs the priority.

Make realistic adjustments in your job and career based on your limitations to avoid exhaustion, collapse, and recurring setbacks. You may cling tenaciously to a particular job or career by sheer will and grit, which challenges you to the limit and leaves you wide open to a world of crises. What happens if the company changes ownership, your job performance demands change, or overtime becomes necessary? These situations affect your job security and destabilize your personal life in other ways as well.

How to Make a Job Shift

To make an effective job shift, do not procrastinate. Move ahead intentionally rather than waiting to be fired or laid off and desperate. The first step in making the shift is to prepare yourself emotionally. Say good-bye to your job before you start the process. A close friend or counselor can help you with this emotional preparation. There are many practical steps you can take to move to a new job.

- Look both at appealing jobs and at those for which you have aptitude. References on self-administered tests of job aptitude are found in Appendix B. You may be failing to use your strengths and depending too heavily on your ability to scramble in your current position. Performing on a job for which you have special aptitude gives you the advantage of higher quality work for the same amount of time and effort.

• Analyze what you cannot do. Determine how much energy you have and how many hours per week you can work. List the reasons that would eliminate a particular type of job as a possibility, such as long hours in a high-stress environment. Consider low-intensity or part-time work.

• Initiate a job search. You can start making inquiries on ads, posting resumes on the Internet, working with an agent, or investigating opportunities by word of mouth.

• Allocate time every day to work on some aspect of your job search. It may take a few weeks or even a few months to find a new job. A common response is to throw your hands up in despair after a few rejections, but you need to persist in your search, by continuously researching, submitting applications or resumes, making calls, and otherwise touching base with friends and work contacts. If you know what you are looking for, chances are good that you will find it, but it takes time, work, and patience. You may also consider "thinking outside the box." Research places that you want to work for and explore how your abilities can fulfill some of their needs. Selling yourself in this way may seem unorthodox, but it can result in a more flexible schedule and environment, and you will be performing tasks that you are good at.

Adjusting your environment to accommodate fibromyalgia often takes low priority. You will need to make your physical health, emotional needs, and your future your first priority.

Now that you have completed Step Three, it is time to move on to Step Four where we guide you through tasks to help you protect what you have built.

6

Step Four:
Stabilize Fibromyalgia
by Managing Stress
and Crises

⊙

You made it to Step Four, and that means that you have done a lot of hard work. Step Four is a critical step that will help you to stabilize your fibromyalgia, protect your accomplishments, and keep the lifestyle changes that you have worked so hard to make. With much effort and care, you have started to set up a new pattern for living your life. However, this new pattern is fragile—it's easy for you to experience setbacks until you put safeguards in place. Setbacks to lower levels of functioning are signified by more than collapse for a day or two. This kind of event is a reversal that sends your living patterns tumbling out of control. Your relationships, job, and/or living arrangements are disrupted. It takes more out of you to recuperate, regroup, rebuild your wounded self-image, and reestablish your place; full recovery takes months and even seasons each time a setback occurs. Setbacks are notoriously common in affecting the FM sufferer and his or her family. They are also almost expected in those who don't know how to protect themselves.

Identifying Causes of Setbacks

People with fibromyalgia usually have little skill in adapting because few of them realize that adapting is even an option. Medication may bring some relief, but added stress, such as not being able to handle certain situations, will counteract the medication. In many cases setbacks arise from stress—FM sufferers are particularly vulnerable to stress and few of them have strong skills in managing it.

The worst news about setbacks is that they tend to recur. Unmanaged FM creates instability, which is why you need skill in adapting to have stability. If you make no progress in learning about adapting, recurring setbacks will likely become your pattern. Thus, you need to make prevention a top priority. One way to do this is to study every setback as it occurs: where does the problem lie, what could I have done to prevent it, and what signs do I need to look for in order stop it before it happens again?

Unfortunately, many people fail to learn from their setbacks. A high frequency of recurring setbacks was recognized by social worker Patricia Fennell, author of the *Chronic Illness Workbook*. She calls them *repeating loops*, a shifting back and forth between the initial struggles and the early phases of adapting to chronic illness. An individual beginning to adjust to a chronic illness may start to achieve a sense of stability. Unfortunately, the situation often does not last, since crises often occur to hinder attempts to adapt. The three main causes of these recurring setbacks—and what can be done about them—are discussed in the following sections.

Lack of Skill in All Areas of Adapting

If you are like most people, you were not born with skills in adapting—you have to learn them. Difficulty with adapting, often in all areas at once, can lead you to have setbacks. Weak adaptation skills can put your entire life in complete opposition to your living situation. Without adjustments, your everyday way of life is competing with FM, creating a constant strain that can lead to lower levels of functioning.

At any step in adapting, you can learn how to prevent setbacks with the help of a counselor. Arrange for ongoing contact—perhaps on an on-call basis. In this way, you maintain access to your counselor for any emergency. It's almost like a family physician remains on call for emergencies. Neglect in multiple domains of living can lead to recurring setbacks, but counseling can get you back on the right track.

GLENDA'S RECURRING SETBACK

Glenda, an FM sufferer, is usually affable and lively in manner, and she receives regular medical care. She worked full-time in the inventory division of a retail firm; however, her employer made constant demands for high-speed performance. Understandably, Glenda did not do well in this work environment and quit, and she made no attempt to locate more suitable work. Glenda's husband, an easygoing repairman, had a sister with a devastating chronic illness and as such is seldom unduly distressed by his wife's periodic downturns. Glenda's relatives from another state visit her about once a year, and they have serious doubts that anyone as chipper as Glenda could really have as much pain and fatigue as she claims to have. Glenda is also estranged from her ex-husband and her child from that marriage.

Glenda has serial setbacks—periods of gloom and worsening of symptoms. She notes that these major flares make her unable to communicate with her friends and relatives because she feels too weary to socialize. She has even had her telephone services turned off, to save on expenses. During these months-long episodes, Glenda spends her time with her house pets, watching television, soaking in the hot tub, and reading books. Only her husband sees these gloomy, subdued states, and he remains unperturbed. He does the shopping and housecleaning without complaint and encourages Glenda the best he can. Glenda's friends and relatives are acutely aware of the shutdowns, and consider her "hiding away" routine. Why do the setbacks keep recurring?

By adapting, Glenda could have fewer downturns. During those she does have, she could remain connected with her friends. Every person with FM experiences tumbles, sometimes even due to changes in weather or the ordinary fluctuations in symptom severity. For Glenda to experience a full-blown hiding-out episode due to a downturn means that she is not adapting.

Glenda has at least two strengths, an understanding husband and satisfactory medical care. However, Glenda's liabilities can be listed as follows:

- She has no work to give her a sense of contributing in a constructive way.
- She does not have a supportive family outside her husband; her closest relatives doubt the veracity of her pain and illness.
- She has few social activities.
- She is cut off from her child by a previous marriage.
- She appears to be reticent about letting others see that she is ill, which suggests that Glenda has not accepted that she has FM and is resentful about having to deal with it.

What, specifically, could Glenda do to help herself? First, she could seek out the missing half of her care by finding a counselor. Among other things, the counselor might be able to help her reestablish contact in some form with her child from her previous marriage. Second, Glenda could probably find a satisfying job if she persisted in a search. Third, she could cultivate a new circle of friends and take measures to make sure she maintained social contact with them. However, even with Glenda's reentry into an active life it is not enough to eliminate her setbacks. She needs to make solid progress in dealing with all the domains of living by navigating all of the Four Steps to Adaptation.

Lack of Social Interaction

Hiding out or being socially isolated is a hallmark sign of failure to adapt. The usual causes for isolation include lack of support from family members, the need for rest, and embarrassment at having a chronic illness. You may seek isolation because you are mortified to let others view you as infirm. To be discounted in this way is a demeaning experience and may lead you to cut yourself off from otherwise close friends.

One technique to overcome social isolation is to stop using the excuse of "waiting until you feel well" to socialize. If you waited for that, you could find yourself a permanent recluse. Another technique is to make sure you have a few close friends to meet with every month or so to avoid withdrawing into yourself and staying shut up in the house. These are exemplary techniques for continuing on the path toward adapting to FM and avoiding one of the common pitfalls of this chronic illness.

Lack of Skill in a Specific Area of Adapting

Without the ability to handle trip-up areas, you and your family are vulnerable to setbacks every time the event occurs. For example, you could be tripped up because of difficulty defusing emotional distress in family members at home or because of inability to defuse stigma in the social environment.

MABEL'S RECURRING SETBACK

Mabel, an FM sufferer in her late thirties, had an outdoor job inspecting equipment. She was on her feet all day and was exhausted at the end of the day. Her FM symptoms grew worse in bad weather and on a heavy schedule. During a major flare-up of her symptoms, she was unable to work anymore; when her pleas for a lighter schedule went unheeded, she quit her job. After several months of rest, her symptoms improved and she sent out her résumé, looking for indoor work. She was offered a job working with equipment in a large building that would not require her to go out-doors. She told us her story.

My work competence was technically good. I could do my work on par with the best of anyone in the department. It was an indoor job and I had to move about to various places with my test equipment. That was great, much less strenuous than working outdoors. But having FM, I was stretched to my limits by working full-time. I did my full share of work, but my workload increased after several people transferred out of the department. After that, my symptoms worsened and I had to take extra medica-tion. My symptoms continued to worsen despite extra medication. Along with the worsening, I began making mistakes on the job, not serious ones, but this was unusual for me. Every day was a strain, and I spent most evenings in despair, often crying. My boss called me in and I had to explain the FM and my need for an adjustment in workload. I was given a lighter load, but my coworkers thought I was getting off easy. They began to rib me. Really, I did my work as well as anyone in the department, and at the minimum I deserved respect for that. Later, they taunted me about my work-load. It was more than I could take. My symptoms became so severe that it was not humanly possible to continue. I felt like a total failure. My only choice was to quit and hope to get disability benefits.

Mabel deserves credit for recognizing the futility of an outdoor job and taking the initiative to find an indoor one. After quitting, she was able to recover and secure yet another job within a year. However, while the indoor job allowed for a margin of safety, it was not enough and the demand for longer hours created a crisis. For a sec-ond time, Mabel faced unwieldy job demands and a succession of stressors includ-ing a decreased ability to perform without mistakes, a call onto the carpet by her boss, and taunting from her coworkers. Her complete setback at the end made work-ing altogether impossible. In both jobs, she was taunted and otherwise stigmatized for having FM as well as clashing with management, all of which led to the loss of her employment.

In Mabel's case, a pattern emerges of stigma formation and discrimination at her workplace and her subsequent infuriation by this treatment. While Mabel's perfor-mance and requests were reasonable, she might have been better able to set cowork-ers at ease. Did she take her coworkers too seriously or take offense unnecessarily? Did she take herself too seriously in demanding respect? Could she have laughed at herself or her coworkers instead? Most people with FM learn skills in normalizing their condition to friends and coworkers. Extra skill in stress management would have also helped Mabel. FM patients constantly face stress, and the repercussions can be disastrous. For that reason, ordinary stress-handling ability is not sufficient for FM people.

However, a setback like this does not spell the end of the road for Mabel. She will need to take time to regroup, overcome despair, rebuild her wounded self-image, rest physically, and recover her health. She can then set up a new way of life for herself by using her past experiences to nurture new skills for the future.

Lack of Skill in Handling Stress

Cumulative stress takes a heavy toll on the FM sufferer. Stress and crises are unpleasant for everyone; however, they pose outright danger for you as an FM sufferer because they can obliterate all of the progress you have made through adaptation. The source of the stress hardly matters. Life with FM is a major source of stress in and of itself. In addition, you and your family have to face life's commonplace events, such as financial setbacks, deaths in the family, or rancorous behavior in coworkers, with a decreased ability to think clearly, keep an even keel, and handle pressure. As your symptoms worsen, so does your mental concentration, while your emotional stability and overall ability to cope decline. Your balance of living is quickly sent spinning out of control.

There is also an increased need for stress-handling skill because your family's living arrangements may not be stable. Your family may be stressed simply by having to put up with FM. Emotions are edgy, and in the wake of unexpected stress, your relationships and living arrangements may take a tumble. Your employment may be only marginally stable—if a new challenge comes up at work, it may threaten your employment.

You have at least some capacity to protect yourself, but is it enough? To be able to lock in your successes in adapting, you will need proficiency in managing stress and crises. You may have a repertoire of skills and be ready to handle the stresses of FM. But if you are like most people, your FM comes first, then the recognition of the needed skills for effective stress/crisis management. Both techniques are discussed in this chapter.

RUTH'S FAMILY: A CRISIS THAT LED TO A SETBACK

Ruth, a wife and a mother with two adolescent children, had suffered FM for many years. A few years ago, her husband developed a back condition. He was able to continue working at the same job, but he became more appreciative of Ruth's illness; as a result, the two became closer emotionally. They worked out an efficient way of doing household chores, recruiting the help of all of their family members. The couple planned family recreation and outings in ways that avoided causing overexertion for either partner.

Then Liz, a troubled niece who was experiencing many social difficulties, moved into the house, and the family was unable to relate to her without becoming embroiled in her problems. Ruth and her family, knowing little about dealing with crises, felt obligated to try to help. Liz and her problems became the new center of attention. The family patterns that Ruth and her husband had worked so hard to set up started to crumble, setting up a family crisis. Within weeks, Ruth's symptoms flared up, and she withdrew from interactions with her family, feeling emotionally undone.

The example of Ruth's family illustrates the need for a wide spectrum of skill in stress management. Skill in dealing with stress pays off for almost anyone, but it pays off doubly well for FM-affected families.

PUTTING SAFEGUARDS INTO PLACE TO PREVENT SETBACKS

If you are in the middle of a setback right now, your best move is to take advantage and analyze it. Reap any lessons it has to teach you. Ordinarily, most people struggle with setbacks without learning from them, which makes recurrences more likely. Your goal is to learn what causes your setbacks so thoroughly that recurrences are unlikely. A counselor can make quite a difference in the amount you learn from a setback. Talking to a professional trained in solving difficulties of this sort can give you a clearer perspective and quicker resolution.

The main safeguards you can adopt for preventing setbacks is to counteract the causes of your setbacks, such as your lack of skill in all areas of adapting, your lack of skill or protection in a specific area of adapting, and your stress vulnerability. Specifically, here are three things to do.

• Graduate from the early dilemmas of fibromyalgia (Steps One and Two). You may still be struggling with denial over the limitations FM imposes on you or still hurting from the losses you have sustained. You may not have established caregiving and care-receiving roles in your family. Perhaps you are still hoping that medical treatment will cure FM. In any of these cases, you are not equipped to deal with FM. Without the proper foundation, your progress can easily be set back. Work on your life-pattern adjustments until you can protect them from toppling over.

• Gain skills in the six domains (Step Three). Learn to detect snags in areas where you have failed to adapt. You can usually identify a strategy to halt these single-snag setbacks.

• Become proficient at defusing stress from all sources. You are not born with the skills you need to defuse stress, but you can learn them with training and practice. Be persistent! Since major life changes are involved, an investment of a few years of training to learn new life skills is not unreasonable.

Specifically, how do you take hold of stress and defuse it? The remainder of this chapter is devoted to showing you these skills. First, you will learn how to detect stress as it arises, before it ever becomes a crisis. Next, you will learn three techniques—strategic planning, deep mental relaxation, and assertiveness training—that you can particularly apply to FM. Finally, you will learn general multimodal management of stress techniques.

HOW TO PREVENT STRESS AND CRISES

One way to defuse stress is to detect it early and nip it in the bud. You need to manage your stress before it manages you. The following three outlooks can interfere with your ability to recognize ongoing stress. If you are able to recognize these outlooks, you can prevent stress early on before it takes over your life.

External Locus of Control

This outlook refers to the belief that your life's events and crises only emerge from forces outside the range of your personal control. In this view, stress management is futile since crises arise from unpredictable human behavior, invisible powers, and a complexity of forces. An internal locus of control will help you to believe that crises arise in part from things over which you do have control. For example, while a driver encounters unpredictable elements on the highway, he or she can avert acci-

THE CYCLE OF STRESSES AND CRISES

Crises rarely arise from a single cause. They are best viewed as difficult episodes coming from a network of contributing causes. By examining these causes, you can see how each of the following components fuels the others and how stress quickly spins out of control to a crisis.

- Precarious or unstable situations with your family, friends, relatives, living environment, employment, and recreation add to . . .
- Emotional overreaction; living without attentiveness; and increasing emotional tension, frustration, or resignation, which add to . . .
- Worries, despair, catastrophizing, loss of hope, unrealistic assumptions, and difficulty defusing painful emotions, which add to . . .
- Loss of initiative and poor planning to take care of your personal needs, which add to . . .
- Fear of people, of social situations, and of speaking up; and fear of going places and of doing things, which add to . . .
- Weak interpersonal skills and lack of confidence, which add to . . .
- Loss of long-term perspective and absence of personal goals as well as difficulty making decisions and taking action, which add to . . .
- Worsening physical symptoms and a diminished ability to cope, which lead to . . .
- A trigger event, that then sets off a crisis of . . .

dents by driving defensively. As an FM sufferer, you and your loved ones will handle stress best by assuming that you can have an internal locus of control—you have control over events in your life.

Living on Automatic Pilot

To live on automatic pilot means that you are using worn-out scripts from the past without taking recent changes into account. In other words, it means that you continue your previous patterns and refuse to make adjustments for the new reality of FM in your life. Living on automatic pilot requires little effort, but it fails to lighten the difficulties of FM because you confront the illness only weakly. Instead, discard old tactics that no longer serve you. You will need introspection and willingness to change to replace the worn-out modes of living with better ways. If you have FM and live on automatic pilot, there will be no chance for growth and adaptation, and your crises will continue to grow.

"Nevermore" Evasion

This last outlook refers to procrastination and, ultimately, the loss of your long-term perspective. If you are stuck in pure wishful thinking—"This is the last time I will ever get into such a jam again"—you are in dangerous denial. You probably do not recognize that your pattern of life is basically one crisis after another. The term *crisis living* is not an exaggeration, as a simple diary of your life over a couple of years would demonstrate. Most FM families alternate between periods of relative calm and stormy episodes. Without FM, stresses and crises take a heavy toll; with FM, these stresses and crises bring worse devastation unless skillful action interrupts the cycle.

TACTICS FOR DEFUSING CRISES

By viewing crises as a network, it is clear that tackling stress vigorously means dealing with it at all accessible points. A single point of attack can never be as effective as a broad range of tactics. To illustrate this multipronged approach, think of a martial arts practitioner who is skilled in a large repertoire of defensive moves, blocks, and parries. When attacked, the martial arts fighter pays close attention and deploys a different set of well-chosen countermoves on each front. Similarly, when you have multiple stresses to deal with, versatility and an arsenal of well-practiced strategies are your best equipment.

Nip Crises Early

Crises start off small and barely recognizable, and then gather momentum. The early stages are where you can cut off a crisis before it gets out of control. To do so requires that you remove or defuse contributors to a crisis long before a trigger event comes along. The trigger event will probably be blamed for the entire eruption, but the contributing factors have been there all along. You usually have plenty of time to deal with various contributing factors before the situation gets out of control. Take preventive action immediately, before any problem has a chance to start.

Sharpen Your Skills in Gauging Stress and Selecting Strategies

Log your stress levels into a private personal journal. In this way, you can record your daily readings—for example, cool, warm, boiling—as a type of stress thermometer. In a detached and objective manner, jot down the sources of stresses. In the same way, without blaming anyone, simply note the contributing factors that add to the network of your stress. As you gain skills in using stress techniques, your thermometer readings should decline. You may also wish to write down the ridiculous suggestions thrown at you, such as "Don't let things get you down," along with your reactions to these statements. Every six months, plot your monthly averages, and watch as your reactions become cooler in temperature.

In addition, write down coping techniques that you currently draw upon, such as gaining cooperation through communication, sticking with your plans, and relaxing to calm your internal stress. Make brief notes in your journal about events in which you have used these techniques. Every three to six months, assess your skill—for example, "novice" or "skilled"—in stress management overall as well as in specific techniques.

STRATEGIES FOR DEALING WITH STRESS

There are many approaches for dealing with stress, but the following techniques have particular success with FM sufferers. Keep your ears and eyes open and you may discover other techniques.

Strategic Planning

Strategic planning calls for a no-excuses, no-holds-barred assault on all known generators of stress in your life. Because you expect stresses, you have the jump on them before they arrive. Some stressful situations might emerge out of the blue, but many are predictable. Thus, you can plan for and manage the predictable ones before they arrive. You can shift commitments, call in resources, and allocate time for rest and recuperation. Strategic planning calls for you to brainstorm to eliminate stress generators so that you do not struggle with them in the first place. You will need to analyze your unrealistic goals, crammed schedule, unrealistic commitments, and overinvolvement in activities. What can you realistically accomplish? What is practical and helpful? What is optional or nonessential?

For example, consider analyzing your job. What are your health requirements for working? What are your aptitudes and capacities to perform the job? Does the job require you to sit motionless for long periods of time, working at a computer? Do you have to carry out repetitive muscular motions? Is there a pressure-cooker environment? You may have to let go of your emotional attachment to your job or career in this ultra-practical realm of strategic planning. Your assignment is to appraise the job and take the necessary actions to minimize stress in this area of your life.

Relaxation

Another method for defusing stress is using deep relaxation. This is the technique of choice to help you achieve detachment and objectivity in dealing with challenges and stresses. Your external circumstances may be in turmoil, but upon entering a state of deep mental relaxation, you can put the outer world aside for the time being. You then experience a refreshing sense of calm that is free of tension, busy thoughts, and distressing emotions. This technique is related to methods used in meditation and self-hypnosis.

If you are successful in using this technique, you will be able to ease your way through situations that would disturb others. Few things can compare to the beatific ease of one of these relaxation states smoothing over your life's stresses. To enter into a deep state of relaxation softens the grip of your involvement with others in stressful situations. It makes you less emotionally dependent on others for achieving a sense of comfort and satisfaction. You become less needy and less dependent and have fewer tendencies to be hurt or upset by others' behavior.

In deep mental relaxation, physical relaxation usually comes first. You may want to start with diaphragmatic breathing. You can also use progressive muscle relaxation, focusing your attention on various muscle groups one after another. As you relax, you calm your mind, your emotions, and eventually the restlessness itself.

There are two categories of inductions, or ways to bring on deep relaxation. One is by feeling your way down into this state, a technique that can only be gained by practice. If your therapist does spoken inductions to induce a state of deep relaxation, you can practice at counseling sessions. The second skill is to learn how to do your own inductions. The help of a counselor is highly recommended if you intend to learn these techniques. After you gain familiarity with these types of inductions, you can learn to do your own, which usually requires audiotapes. Your counselor may make tapes for you and allow you to keep them. You may also write out your own inductions and then record them using your own voice. An advantage to using your own tapes is that you encounter less resistance or guardedness; after all, you are listening to your own voice and your own suggestions about dismissing outer thoughts and entering an inwardly peaceful state. A disadvantage is that it is difficult to surprise yourself with your induction. Surprise is an effective tool in induction, and it can be recovered to a degree by allowing time to pass before listening to a tape you have recorded. If you have forgotten some of the induction, you can experience a partial element of surprise as you listen.

Deep mental relaxation can also help control pain. In most instances, training, practice, and experience are needed, but this technique has definite potential to help you manage your pain. In a deep state of relaxation, your pain may subside. Or the pain may remain as a sensation that is detached from who you are, leaving you untouched or less touched by pain. In some self-hypnosis states, sensations of pain can be altered. For example, as painful stimuli are perceived they are converted to warmth or heat by concentrating on these sensations. Pain can also be utilized as motivation to drive the relaxation state deeper; deeper states are more detached from your bodily sensations and more attuned to your inner state of gentle calm.

Assertiveness Training

Face-on confrontation of stress has a prominent place among approaches for people with FM for two reasons. First, if you are like many FM people, you have difficulty with assertiveness, and second, you need to be assertive to protect your health. Being assertive protects you from impositions from others and from overcommitment, thereby guarding your health. For example, your friends may assume that you have abundant energy, like them, and are not attuned to the precautions that apply to you.

Unfortunately, we have found that many people with FM do not deem themselves equal to others in important ways:

- They don't expect people to give them equal and fair treatment.

- They allow people to take advantage of them without protest.

- They feel guilty when not responding to needs or demands from others.

For example, have your friends or relatives ever asked you to go on an extended trip with them? If so, did they understand the sacrifices and misery the trip could cause you, or did they ignore the limitations imposed on you by FM? More important, did you feel free to set limits without feeling alienated from them? Were you able to assert your needs firmly but pleasantly? To do so enables you to protect your health while maintaining your friendships.

Assertiveness is not aggressiveness, arrogance, or domineering behavior. It means insisting on receiving the same consideration that every person automatically should have. Normally, concessions for ill people are greater than for healthy people, although healthy people expect special consideration if they get sick. If it is normal and right for them, then it is normal and right for you. To save your sanity, simply accept that many people will be insensitive, so that you don't easily become upset about the inconsideration of others. No matter how ill you are or how clearly you have already explained yourself, some will fail to notice. Never mind—calmly but firmly tell them again. To do so in this manner is a health-conserving practice that is as potent as any medication. To be assertive enough, you may have to make emotional adjustments. After the onset of fibromyalgia, you may become more needy and struggle to please friends who fill your emotional needs. Correcting the emotionally needy position by getting support from a variety of sources and improving your sense of self-worth allows you to project the right degree of assertiveness.

It is important to remember that assertiveness works best if you speak with directness. In most instances, directness is served by honesty, meaning that you say what is true even at the risk of not pleasing others. It's okay to say to someone, "My energies are limited and I am already committed. I wish I could help, but my own health must come first." However, sometimes a situation requires a more vigorous assertion of your rights. If you are being nudged or pushed into something that you prefer to not be involved with, a firm assertion is in order: "I'm committed elsewhere; I'm not interested." If someone still makes demands on your interest and energies, you can make your assertion firmer: "No, I don't need to be involved in your project. Where I place my interest is my decision." If you need a sharp assertion to a would-be friend making an excessive demand, you might say, "Who are you to push me into doing things I do not wish to do?"

Remember that learning to manage your stress is hardly different from learning to manage your life. Learning a spectrum of skills makes it possible for you to handle many of life's problems. The skills in the following examples can contribute to the endeavor of coping and adapting to your daily life.

Behavioral Management

Action can shape your thoughts and feelings. Thus, success in carrying out a constructive action imparts confidence and dispels your fears about doing the action. A technique for dispelling fear could be rehearsals of graded task assignments where real-life situations are used. For example, you dislike getting out and going places. Your assignment might be to gradually increase leaving your home and going on errands. You make progress in small steps, finding that you can accomplish first a part of the task you once dreaded and then the entire task.

Emotional Management

Emotional management as a technique requires such mental work as paying attention to specific emotions. For example, if you have a problem with anger management, you would work to develop a sensitive awareness of anger as it arises. Then you would note the eliciting event that precedes the anger. Thus, you accurately label the emotion and reappraise the event. Your counselor may then add additional techniques, such as self-talk and relaxation. Self-talk is how you talk to yourself. FM people are often very critical of themselves and they need to stop the negative self-talk and start the positive. One way of improving your self-worth is through positive affirmations, which are a type of self-talk.

Sensations

Your sensations of tension and stress can be managed by several different means. One is biofeedback. In biofeedback, your therapist tapes electrodes to your forehead muscles or to other muscles. You then watch the electrical voltage readings coming from these muscles and learn to bring the voltage and tension down. It really can be done! Massage is another way in which your body sensation can produce total relaxation. You may also wish to use techniques such as tai chi, a very gentle technique of rhythmic movements, to produce mental relaxation and stress reduction.

Guided Imagery

Guided imagery is highly effective in managing anticipated stressful events. Using imagery, you can preview events before they occur. You can rehearse a life change, a major move, or a separation from a close friend by this method. You then reach satisfying resolutions without living through the actual situation. When the actual situation occurs, you have already resolved it emotionally.

For example, suppose you are being forced to leave your present home and living arrangement. You might reduce the resulting aggravation and stress by rehearsing the move using guided imagery. Your therapist might ask you to imagine the move into your new home: how comfortable it is, what it looks like, what the new kitchen feels like, what dinner is like in the new dining room, and what it feels like on the new outdoor patio. Even if the rooms in your new place are not the same as the ones you imagined, you have laid to rest the tension of the move before it even takes place.

Cognitive Approaches

Cognitive, or mental, approaches are used extensively in counseling to correct irrational beliefs that amplify stress. If your mental images are distorted, your emotions are likely to be distressed. Correcting cognitive distortions, then, is the central theme of this approach. If you are like most individuals, you may bend reality to a degree, often toward the pessimistic side. By correcting your assessments so that they accurately fit the reality, your distress can be diminished. An important thing to note is that an overly positive or optimistic view can also be ruinous if it runs counter to reality. For example, it would be excessively optimistic to have high expectations about someone you have just met. Likewise, irrational, unfounded hopes could plunge you into crushing disappointment. Wholesome emotions almost always have their basis in a clear grasp of reality. For more information on this topic, as well as on the value of confronting and reversing overoptimism, look at *The Positive Power of Negative Thinking* by J. K. Norem.

Interpersonal Relations

Interpersonal stress management techniques include assertiveness training, communication skills training, negotiating, friendship and intimacy training, and social skills training. A very effective technique in interpersonal relations is role-play. In role-playing, you may try out various approaches to a problem—usually with the help of a therapist. For example, you and your spouse may try switching roles. Your spouse imagines what it feels like getting up in the morning feeling unrefreshed and having terrible neck pain. He or she practices how to ask for help with the early morning hustle of getting ready for work and making breakfast. The FM person will fill in the other person's role and try to imagine waking up feeling rested and without pain and being able to leisurely have breakfast. Role-playing is a powerful way to work out interpersonal relations so that they are more comfortable for everyone involved.

Biological Factors

Biological factors are probably the most obvious therapy on this list as they include medical measures. While medical treatment does not eradicate fibromyalgia, you should optimize it as much as possible. Regular exercises, such as stretching, limbering, and pool exercises are highly recommended. In addition, sound nutrition, regular sleep, avoidance of overexertion, and healthy practices in general will contribute to your successful management of stress.

When stresses and crises send your fibromyalgia spinning out of control, your ability to handle stress declines—right at the key time when you need a surplus of these skills. You therefore need an abundance of stress-management skills for protection as you and your family set up new patterns of living. By gaining this skill in Step Four, you can now move forward in creating a fulfilling life by learning about and eliminating barriers that impede your progress.

7

REMOVING BARRIERS TO ADAPTATION

◉

Barriers—blocks, entanglements, and psychological traps—often impede your ability to adapt. While barriers do not pertain to all people who are affected with fibromyalgia, they affect the large majority. To ensure that you make forward progress in adapting, it is likely that you will need to remove, or correct, some barriers. While a barrier may feel like a failure, being able to detect it gives you an edge and a chance to disentangle yourself from it. Ideally, once you have discovered each barrier, you will be able to prevent it from ever holding back your progress again.

In this chapter, you will learn about the most common types of barriers that people encounter. Some of these barriers may have existed before the onset of your FM. Interestingly, one particular barrier, the people-pleaser trait, is prominent among people with FM. You can use the descriptions of these common barriers to identify which ones affect you individually and to begin working on them immediately. You can simultaneously try to identify barriers as you begin your work with the Four Steps to Adaptation. Remember, too, that while both you and your loved ones face barriers they will probably be different kinds.

As you did in identifying common reactions to FM in Step One and common setbacks in Step Four, your task is to go through the descriptions of each barrier, find out which ones pertain to you, and focus on overcoming these specific barriers.

IDENTIFYING COMMON BARRIERS TO ADAPTATION

A brief overview of common barriers appears first with a more detailed description of each as well as effective techniques for overcoming them follows.

- Treatable emotional conditions are problems such as clinical depression and anxiety that hinder your adapting but are readily treatable.

- The people-pleaser trait is such a strong compulsion to please and help others that it creates difficulty setting limits and is a detriment to your own health and progress.

- A situational impasse refers to rigid circumstances—for example, your finances, living environment, relationships, or job—beyond your control that block your progress.

- Caregiver, or support-giver, stress includes physical exhaustion with depression, emotional exhaustion with indifference, and emotional overreaction on the part of your loved one, resulting in such things as anger and misplaced blame.

- The overdone support role is a barrier that arises when your support person does literally everything for you, disallowing you to make a constructive contribution to your family.

- The helpless victim trap is when you feel despair, outrage, victimhood, ruination, an overwhelming loss of your sense of self-worth, a fear of taking the initiative, and a sense of fury and blame toward others.

- The caregiver-victim dual trap happens when the "victim"—the FM sufferer—manipulates and controls the caregiving members of his or her family based on a sense of victimhood and entitlement. The primary caregiver and family members appease your demands and in doing so empower you in a domineering role.

Treatable Emotional Conditions

The emotional conditions included in the group of treatable emotional conditions are clinical depression, panic disorder, anxiety disorder, and bipolar disorder (formerly called manic-depressive disorder). It also includes the disorders of extreme stress, which are caused by childhood abuse, spousal abuse, verbal abuse, molestation, rape, assault, witnessing brutal violence, combat in war, and similar experiences. In dealing with this emotional barrier, line up all of the help you can get for your battle with fibromyalgia. Have your doctor and counselor check for emotional conditions that could hamper your progress.

Clinical depression may emerge due to suffering from illness. In addition, FM itself—its chemistry and the altered circuitry of brain neurons—may predispose a person to mood changes. In some cases, your genetic make-up may predispose you to depression. How do you tell the difference between merely feeling sad and clinical depression? Here are things your physician and counselor will be looking for:

- Severely depressed mood

- Decreased interest in previously engaging activities

- Decreased ability to make decisions

- Feelings of worthlessness

- Diminished ability to concentrate

- A sense of moving in slow motion

- Recurrent thoughts of death or plans for death

- Sleep abnormalities and loss of energy, which also occurs with FM

Help in treating these emotional conditions makes your main struggle with FM easier. If you are like many FM sufferers, you may hesitate getting help for treatable emotional conditions. Perhaps you hesitate out of denial. Failure to obtain support in this area, however, makes adjusting to your illness more difficult. If taking the right medication can ease your life, waste no time and use all the help available to you. You may avoid seeing a doctor out of fear of what the medication will do to you. Your doctor should be monitoring your medication, and you should be keeping track of any side effects. If side effects occur be sure to let your doctor know so the dose or medication can be adjusted.

The People-Pleaser Trait

The people-pleaser trait is a facet of personality, not a mental illness. The main feature of this trait is a compulsion to please others by putting their needs in front of your own. If you have this condition, you even risk your own emotional and physical health and progress in adapting. You probably do not even realize that you are neglecting your most basic self-maintenance tasks—eating, sleeping, seeking medical care, and taking medications. As a people pleaser, you have enormous difficulty setting limits, maintaining priorities, and saying "no" when needed. Of course, there is nothing wrong with bringing authentic help to others. But it is dangerous to be so self-sacrificing that it interferes with taking care of your own needs.

A telltale feature of this trait is when you find yourself molding your life to the ideals, desires, strivings, or images of your loved ones, specifically your close family members. In doing so, you neglect or push aside your own desires and aspirations. You may also be heavily involved with others outside the home, assisting, advising, encouraging, and pulling your friends out of problems. You may feel that if you don't make the effort to help, you couldn't live with yourself.

People pleasing is a physically and emotionally draining compulsion. Combine this with the symptoms of FM, and you do not have energy left to take care of yourself or carry out your family roles. However, the people-pleasing trait can often be traced to a time long before the onset of FM. Some people in our support groups report having been made to feel degraded and worthless in the early years of their lives. The result is that they will do anything they can to attain, restore, or maintain a sense of personal worthiness. For them, winning others' gratitude is important for their self-worth.

Although the people-pleaser trait is exceedingly common in fibromyalgia patients, it is not currently viewed as part of the FM syndrome because some individuals with FM do not have this trait and because, in most cases, it preexisted the onset of FM symptoms. However, the people-pleaser trait seriously blocks progress in adapting. Few people with this mind-set can organize themselves enough to get to Step Two. They remain stuck at a relatively low level of functioning until they can overcome it.

There are two routes to overcoming such strong, compulsive behavior. The first is good communication and a healthy relationship with your loved ones, both of which can help you take better care of yourself. The second is professional counseling, which can help you avoid behaviors that are detrimental to you, your health, and your goals. The people-pleaser trait is a serious and common problem, and it can be overcome.

MARGARET'S STORY: OVERCOMING THE PEOPLE-PLEASER TRAIT

Margaret, an FM sufferer from our support groups, immediately recognized that "people pleasing" described her mode of relating for many years. As a result, she has been in long-term counseling to overcome this compulsion. Her story follows in her own words.

I always tried to please my friends. It bothered me deeply if I failed to help when asked or to come through when needed. My friends often wanted me to do something that would aggravate my FM, maybe go visiting in a town a few hours away. I knew the price I would have to pay but hardly ever said no. Maybe part of it was simply the wish to belong and to not be rejected by friends. But there is another part, too, a drive to get involved even when it would make better sense to let others solve their own problems.

Before I was married I tried to help down-and-out people. I even loaned them money. Some tried to pull me into absurd schemes, and they seldom used the money that I gave them to get themselves on track. None of them repaid me a cent. It also meant I overextended myself financially. I was too much of an "easy touch" to take care of my own needs! Much of this tendency came from my parents, especially my mother. Mother was rarely pleased by anything we did, and so we put extra effort into every task trying to please her and gain bits of acceptance. It was never good enough, and I don't remember getting praise. Years later, it was like my life didn't belong to me or as if I didn't have my own matters to attend to. My private pursuits stopped whenever the opportunity came up to gain someone's appreciation, affections, and praise. I just wanted to be liked and appreciated and was always eager to help.

My first marriage was a disaster because of this. In looking back, I wonder how I could have married someone who does not give anything to you, who only wants to take from you and have control over you. I realized that I had married a selfish and controlling person. I was a giver and he was a taker. Things were his way or no way! It was easy for him to win in my case because I did not even know how to put up a fight. On the contrary, I attempted to keep the peace and help him get along with my family and friends. So I was always giving in, but never got anything in return. His behavior became more callous and controlling—not caring about my welfare, feelings, or safety. Eventually my friends saw it and urged me to cease this, to wake up and do something. I was afraid of confronting him and standing up for myself, so I started going to a counselor for help. This helped me to realize that I didn't have to live that way any longer.

After some years in counseling, I realized that I was worthy of being valued and loved for myself, not for what I could do for others. I didn't need to grovel for approval. I met Roy, a quiet man with depth of character, and we got married. This time I just accepted my worthiness to be loved as a given; I did not try to make myself deserving of love and acceptance. Some men might have seen FM as a flaw that decreased my worth. But Roy and I never saw it that way. We see FM as joint property that came with the marriage, so he is very supportive. It is a loving relationship, but it took me a long time to accept love in this manner.

The people-pleaser trait in Margaret's earlier life drained her to the detriment of her physical and emotional health. In her first marriage, Margaret gained satisfaction by appeasing her husband. He gained satisfaction by dominating or winning out over her. As expected, this kind of arrangement cannot bring lasting satisfaction. Nevertheless, Margaret felt ambivalent about bailing out. After all, to please him brought comfort to her wounded sense of self-worth, despite the downside. Her solution was to clear away her own problem through counseling. Not every marriage with a people pleaser is doomed from the start, as a husband with integrity would have given Margaret the full respect she deserves as a person. After clearing away the people-pleaser trait in counseling, she sought a new relationship in which there would be mutual respect.

Margaret needed the help of a counselor to overcome her people-pleasing trait because the trait seems to have a mind of its own. It runs a person's life and cannot be switched on and off at will. To confront it turns it into an internal battle, but to have a counselor is to have a strong ally in this battle.

Situational Impasses

In some instances, you cannot make forward progress because of difficult circumstances restricting the way. These may be financial constraints, relationships that won't budge, emotional entanglements, or obligations toward ill or dependent relatives. Difficult circumstances can block adaptation despite your best efforts. The variations of situational impasses are endless and unique to each situation. If you are caught in this block, the following suggestions may help you.

- Brainstorm your situation with a counselor. Search for exits.

- Be sure to not contribute to an impasse. For example, you might encourage entrapment by your willingness to be an emotional hostage or victim, or you may feel too paralyzed by guilt to make the lunge to freedom.

- Maintain hope as your circumstances can change and you can then move on.

- Prepare mentally and materially for your exit. Make connections that could be useful to you later. Save up resources that could come in handy.

- Know and envision your goals for your life. Move toward them even in small ways when the opportunity arises.

Caregiver Stress

If you are a support person, your progress in adapting may be blocked by personal traits or conditions having nothing to do with your loved one's illness. The losses and stresses set off by FM can also cause you to revert to a lower level of functioning. As a support person, you can become overloaded with stress in simply performing the tasks of mechanical, or instrumental, care, such as household chores and errands. Providing emotional support for a person demoralized by FM can be even more demanding. And finally, the loss of emotional satisfaction from your spouse, who was once a fountain of comfort can unleash anger or sometimes even rage. There are three types of variants on support-giver stress that create barriers in providing support for your FM partner.

Physical Exhaustion with Depression. Support-giver stress syndrome arises out of sheer exhaustion and depression from the physical demands of providing instrumental care—household chores, errands, assistance with dressing and bodily care, preparation of meals, and other mechanical tasks. Providing this care is sometimes viewed as a "martyr" situation. In providing extensive hands-on care, which is sometimes strenuous and often time consuming, your energies get overextended; your workload exceeds the level you can handle without feeling stressed; and, as a result, you become exhausted, depressed, lethargic, and frustrated. In addition, you are sacrificing time that you previously used for rest and personal recreation. This problem is most commonly encountered when the physical dependency needs of your partner are so great that no other family member or helper is available to provide you with a respite.

In these cases, your health, well-being, and ability to function can be wiped out. To avoid physical exhaustion, you must attend to your own self-care. The following list includes standard recommendations for people providing care for a chronically ill individual.

- Continue to get regular exercise and rest and to eat a good diet.

- Make sure you get respites and breaks if you are providing continuous care.

- Do not hesitate to ask for help from others who are close.

- If possible, hire domestic help such as a housekeeper.

- Maintain your contacts with friends and associates; avoid isolating yourself.

- Maintain at least some hobbies and interests that do not require the participation of your loved one and that provide you with an independent source of satisfaction.

- Get medical attention and counseling for signs of clinical depression.

NICOLAS'S STORY: HANDLING PHYSICAL EXHAUSTION

Nicolas was blindsided as fibromyalgia started to affect his wife and active companion, Barbara. At first, Nicolas disregarded the new illness, thinking that it would pass. But when his wife starting going to doctors for help, he quickly became involved and led his family in adapting to FM. Barbara has told us, "Without Nicolas, I would have been lost. I would never have come through this with a happy life." At the onset of Barbara's FM, the couple's two daughters were ten and twenty years old. Nicolas worked regular hours for a commercial airline company. Barbara worked full-time for a surgical supply firm providing in-home services to customers. Eventually, Barbara had to stop working full-time.

Nicolas describes how he dealt with caregiver stress:

Our younger daughter and I pitched in to do the extra work. In my own family, if someone was ill, we would take turns providing care. If you don't have a sense of family, if everyone is out only for themselves, then one person can get stuck with the whole job. If you have to help her with bathing, dressing, and eating, it is a huge job and is too much for one person. Barbara, though, could still dress herself, prepare meals, put clean clothes in the closet, and do other light things. The remainder of the tasks my daughter and I handled fine. I did not neglect my hobbies. I continued jogging. Barbara insisted that I keep it up even without her. I also enjoyed carving models of ships. So I was able to continue my recreations.

Emotional Exhaustion with Indifference. While physical conditions can cause caregiver stress, as a support person you will more commonly feel strain arising from emotional demands. To provide emotional support for your spouse who is suffering from a chronic illness can be wearing and lead to utter exhaustion. Unending demands for you to be supportive to someone who is demoralized with pain and fatigue can take a heavy toll on you. Counselors can help with this by teaching you skills that you need to provide emotional support. It is also helpful to identify additional ways of finding emotional satisfaction, such as developing hobbies, watching movies, having friends over, taking respites, and practicing deep relaxation, that will supplement your current sources of satisfaction.

Nicolas's Advice: Dealing with Emotional Exhaustion

Nicolas offers the following advice if you are emotionally exhausted from trying to bring cheer to a suffering, demoralized person who lives in pain and fatigue.

Because of my earlier family experiences, I was already familiar with this territory. I can say, briefly, that if you want to keep your family together and close, you cannot run away from the emotional part. To run away is to disconnect. Families can become disconnected if a member experiences pain and suffering. These are not favorite topics and family members tend to run away. But even if you back away from things like that, how can you believe you will never face pain and illness in your own life? No one is exempt from experiencing pain. None of us can arrange to live only in sunshine and fair weather. Nobody is immune to growing old or coming down with an illness. Refusal to look at these matters only postpones your work. In the long haul, you have to deal with them. If you try to insulate yourself from the trials your spouse is going through, you will become estranged from him or her. Vice versa, nothing could be more comforting for your loved one than for you to be there and have intimate knowledge of what he or she is going through.

Emotional Overreaction. As a support person, you also may experience devastating emotional distress because your spouse, once a veritable fountain of comfort and satisfaction, is currently unable to give you these things. This barrier tends to happen when the impact of this loss is unexpected because you mistakenly think that you are strong enough to handle these feelings on your own. Eventually, you will feel overwhelming confusion and anger, becoming enraged and blaming your spouse for creating problems. You feel overwhelmed with anger, resentment, misplaced blame, cynicism, bitterness, and disappointment. Once your anger erupts, it is best to seek professional help. Immediate counseling can help you and your loved one reestablish emotional give and take on the part of both of you. You can resolve this once you and your spouse recognize that help is needed and take appropriate action.

The Overdone Support Role

If you are like some support givers, you may relish the role and end up doing literally everything for your spouse. However, this can be an obstacle in adapting. You expect your partner to do nothing and to have no designated roles that she is responsible for performing. This overdone support role backfires because you have deprived your spouse of all roles, many of which could strengthen her sense of self-worth. Your partner becomes a passive recipient of care, unable to make a constructive contribution to your family, leading her to feel helpless, useless, or like a burden or liability. It is an insult to her real capacities and willingness to make a meaningful contribution. Few people can feel worthwhile with no roles or responsibilities. FM reduces the number of roles that a person can perform, but to let it remove all roles leads to a helpless dependency.

The overdone support role, however, may turn out to be not a block but a stage that leads to more mature role arrangements. If your partner finds that he lacks any means of making constructive contributions, he may look for ways to make these contributions. You and your spouse can work out roles that he can perform that permit him the satisfaction of making a contribution.

NICOLAS'S ADVICE: AVOIDING THE OVERDONE SUPPORT ROLE
Nicolas shares the following example about how he avoided the overdone support role trap.

You cannot step in with a heavy hand and take away all of a person's roles. I might dislike the idea that household chores cause Barbara pain and tiredness. But despite my concerns, she does a few chores. My belief is that everyone needs a function, a place to make a contribution. No one is satisfied without some role. Let me give an example. I'm perfectly willing to clean the kitchen, bathroom, or any other part of the house. Just to prove it, I scrub the dirtiest room in the house so Barbara won't forget that I'm willing. But I know she likes to clean the bathrooms. That's her nature. If I took that totally away from her, it would strike a blow to her sense of usefulness. She pays a modest price for doing one or two bathrooms. But it carries meaning for her, and I don't interfere.

The Helpless Victim Trap

The helpless victim trap resembles a recurring setback except that your sense of despair deepens and feeds on itself. Despair becomes a trap, a vortex that pulls you further downward. Many factors may contribute to this situation, including weak coping skills at the outset of FM or past episodes, perhaps from your early years, of living in detestable or abusive circumstances. There are three variants of the helpless victim trap—a sense of despair and helplessness, a sense of victimhood, and the dramatic victim response.

A Sense of Despair and Helplessness. Michelle, a married FM sufferer with a family and a daytime job, made appointments with her doctor, who prescribed several medicines to alleviate her FM symptoms. The symptoms were eased by the medications but were by no means under control. Michelle became increasingly irritable and lashed out at the other members of her family. Soon her family lost patience and lashed back at her. Michelle's anguish and distress became intense and the situation brought back vivid memories of harsh childhood experiences. She recalled that when she tried to express herself, she was ignored and then reprimanded for complaining. The all-too-human reaction of despair set in, and Michelle gradually stopped doing almost everything meaningful in her life: working, going places, making time for play and hobbies, seeing old friends, and making new friends. She ended up with no family roles and no constructive outlets, isolated in her house feeling deserted and miserable. She began to feel powerless and completely dependent on others. Her sense of self-worth plummeted.

This trap is difficult because the more you shrink from the practical world and shun decisions and action; the more powerless you feel to deal with things. As you agonize over your predicament, you sink further into despair. Your pain, fatigue, and other symptoms also worsen.

If you have feelings of helplessness and despair, a counselor may send you to someone for antidepressant medication. In addition, your counselor will help you uncover the causes of your sense of defeat and worthlessness and then work with you on building your self-confidence by focusing on your past successes and finding things that you are still capable of doing.

Sense of Victimhood. Life can be terribly unfair. Even if you have led a kind life, you may still be suffering cruelly from illness. But the victim mentality helps nothing; it only adds to your sense of hopelessness. To overcome a sense of victimhood, it is important to understand that everyone who has fibromyalgia has struggled with their sense of self-worth after seeing what FM does to them. All FM sufferers have also succumbed at times to seeing themselves as victims. Everyone thinks they deserve a little compassion from others or maybe some special consideration. But calling yourself "ruined victim" or "damaged goods" borders on self-disparagement. Doing so needlessly discredits yourself.

To combat your sense of victimhood, answer the following questions:

- Although I am affected by FM and less functional than before, can I retain my sense of dignity?

- In my view, can I remain intact at least in personhood?

- On behalf of myself and of others with FM, can I advocate realistic self-acceptance?

This last stance allows you to be as functional as possible, ensuring that your self-image does not drift into a sense of ruin and worthlessness.

The Dramatic Victim Role. A sense of being hurt and thwarted by illness can unleash a storm of outrage. In this variant of the helpless victim trap, the mood exhibited is fury. You lash out with accusations, strewing blame for your plight on anyone who is near. A dilemma of being the dramatic victim is that your friends, acquaintances, and health-care providers soon become antagonized. You may not be able to establish long-term care because of confrontations and clashes with your providers, which leads to frequent switches in health-care practitioners.

Another problem is that in playing the dramatic victim, you may create problems for other people with FM by drawing attention to yourself. Perhaps you show up at support groups and monopolize the meeting or leave an unforgettable impression in a doctor's office or pharmacy. Some onlookers, having encountered such spectacles, unfairly stereotype all people with FM based on this behavior when only a small percentage of FM patients react this way. If you are one of these individuals, your behavior may be a cry for intensive psychiatric treatment in addition to treatment for the chronic pain and fatigue. To work on changing this behavior and to continue your progress, you need to seek a psychiatrist or counselor.

The Caregiver-Victim Dual Trap

In the caregiver-victim trap, both you and your partner are trapped together; in many cases, your entire family falls into the trap. It begins when the FM sufferer is convinced that she deserves special entitlements. You prefer to give the orders, to compel others to do what you say. The caregiver trap evolves further when, due to an overwhelming sense of compassion or obligation, your loved one gives in to your demands and provides the extra attention you desire. Finally, your friends and other family members unknowingly contribute to the trap by conceding to the victim's demands and trying to be kind. If your loved ones do not cater to your demands and avoid overdoing helping roles, the dual trap will not develop. However, once the new helper roles become the norm for the family, and you continue issuing commands, your family will become subservient, frustrated, resentful, and exhausted.

So how do you and your partner get out of the dual trap? Since you are both emotionally invested in the trap, you both need therapy. A counselor will explore for similar patterns in both your and your partner's early lives that could influence your current relationship. The counselor will also help you both set boundaries. Only then can you establish realistic giving and receiving roles. Such a situation is difficult, but it is not hopeless, especially if both you and your spouse commit yourselves to the healing process. Given a willingness to change and an earnest desire for a loving relationship, you and your loved one can achieve forgiveness, renewal, and new steps to maturity.

ALICE'S STORY: FALLING INTO THE CAREGIVER-VICTIM DUAL TRAP
Alice, a woman whose mother developed fibromyalgia, describes how the caregiver-victim dual trap evolved for her.

My mother was forty-two years old when she came down with FM, and my own symptoms back then were still mild. My father adored her. She was a very lovely lady, always at the center of attention, but her pride and self-image were hit hard by the

FM. She had always loved going to social gatherings and was often the life of the party, but now she could hardly do anything. She was deeply hurt by this turn of events. My father did everything he could to console and please her. We all pitched in to help, my whole family. Father encouraged us to be extra helpful. Mother was so miserable that it made us feel uncomfortable. Gradually she expected and demanded that we be better helpers. We submitted to it because we felt sympathy for her suffering. If we did not respond as she wanted, we increased her suffering and felt terrible. And what standards she required us to meet! If we didn't get the kitchen just right, perfectly clean, she was all over us, and we felt guilty. After all, she couldn't do anything herself, but she did enjoy giving orders. She had us all under her thumb, but we loved her so much we put up with it.

Some time passed, and my father isolated himself. He showed great devotion but was emotionally exhausted. Out of a sense of duty, he took excellent care of my mother, did everything for her, and took her everywhere she wanted to go. Between us, we did all the housework, errands, everything possible to please. We recalled how she had taken care of us growing up. She refused any form of counseling, pain management, or treatment for her condition. This affected her ability to relate to others in a normal manner. In thinking back on the situation, my father must not have been a happy man. He was very devoted, though, and perhaps he was a martyr, but he never complained.

My mother became increasingly bitter, impatient, and hard to please over the years. It was impossible to do enough to make her happy. She lost faith in her lifelong friends and avoided them. She refused offers that could have helped her feel better. Her decision to refuse medical care for FM and for other areas was very discouraging to everyone who loved her. Sadly we watched her decline. She finally died of causes not related to FM.

In Alice's family, drastic shifts occurred in family roles. The FM sufferer managed to put herself into a dominating position. She learned how to play on others' sympathy and use guilt to get her way. She became intimidating to those around her. Her husband, daughter, and other family members assumed subservient roles and sacrificed themselves daily to provide her with the care she wanted. But how did Alice and her family members feel? Anybody looking at the situation from the outside might admire Alice's father for his uncomplaining self-sacrifice. He may have felt like a pressure cooker inside, but he was apparently determined to make the best of the situation.

The shift in roles is key for the development of the full-blown caregiver-victim trap. If family members can maintain realistic boundaries—"here is how much I can offer, no more"—the trap will not develop.

This chapter has helped you to identify the barriers that are preventing you from successfully completing the Four Steps to Adaptation. For the barriers that apply to you, examine and implement the techniques that are useful for resolving them. By doing this, you can expect rapid progress in navigating the Four Steps.

Chapter 8 offers a synopsis of the Four Steps to assist those who suffer from fibro fog.

8

SUMMARY OF THE
FOUR STEPS

◉

Now that you have visited each of the Four Steps to Adaptation as well as the barriers you may need to overcome, the work ahead needs to be framed into a single panoramic view. Chapter 8 is a synopsis, or map, of the tasks of adapting, which is a system that allows for wide individual variation in starting points and in choices of route. Indeed, your exact route will be unique, depending on your situation and personal tendencies. We include real-life excerpts from the stories of two individuals—an FM sufferer with outstanding adaptation techniques and a caregiver with excellent supportive techniques—which may give you some ideas on how to make the Four Steps work for you.

The most practical approach is in an orderly, systematic manner. If you are like most adapters, you will work on more than one step at a time, and you may backslide now and then. When this happens, simply go back and rework the tasks that are appropriate.

STEP ONE: ASSESS YOUR REACTIONS
TO FIBROMYALGIA

Once you have a diagnosis focus on learning as much about the disease as you can, and pay attention to your emotional reactions. This is life altering for you and your loved ones; take time alone, with your partner, and then as a family to share and connect.

To begin adapting to fibromyalgia, you and each of your family members must appraise your reactions to receiving this devastating diagnosis. Common reactions among newly diagnosed FM people and their families:

- Denial

- Supernormalizing

- Sense of worthlessness

- Guilt

- Hello losses—losses in function that can't be relegated to the past

If you are a support person, your first reaction may be denial. Additional reactions for both of you may include:

- A frenzied search for a quick and pleasing answer

- Grief over good-bye losses—cherished things that cannot be brought into the future

At Step One many FM sufferers experience blocks or traps, barriers to forward progress, such as:

- People-pleaser trait

- Helpless victim trap

- Situational impasses

As the support person, you can experience caregiver stress, which manifests itself as:

- Physical exhaustion with depression

- Emotional exhaustion with indifference

- Emotional overreaction with anger and misplaced blame

- Overdone support role

You and your partner may encounter certain blocks together:

• Treatable emotional conditions, such as depression and anxiety

• The caregiver-victim dual trap

By appraising your reactions, you strip away your misperceptions and see FM reduced to its stark reality. This reality boils down to good-bye losses and hello losses. Resolve good-bye losses, such as the loss of friends, your former work, and your way of living, through the mourning process. Even though the losses sustained by support people are somewhat different in character, you also resolve them through the mourning process.

Resolving hello losses, persisting symptoms plus decreases in your ability to function, is difficult; you can't just leave them behind because you are reminded of them daily. To resolve hello losses, you need to plan, and then take action in order to restore your quality of living.

• Task One: Appraise—identify, acknowledge, understand—your reactions to FM.

• Task Two: Resolve your reactions to FM by dismantling them—good-bye losses and hello losses.

• Task Three: Resolve good-bye losses through the mourning process.

• Task Four: Resolve hello losses by planning for the future and taking action.

• Task Five: Appraise barriers.

• Task Six: Resolve barriers.

JOANNE'S STORY: THE IMPORTANCE OF THE EARLY APPRAISAL OF FIBROMYALGIA

Joanne is an experienced administrator and counselor who had to give up her career because of FM. When the symptoms of FM started incapacitating her six years ago, she consulted a number of doctors before being given the correct diagnosis. Medical treatment for FM, though, did not save her career. At her doctor's prompting, she reconsidered her hectic but rewarding career and took an early retirement. Joanne quickly came to grips with FM and successfully adapted to it. Her rapid adaptation is exceptional but not unique. It demonstrates one manner of successful dealings with FM, incorporating the kinds of lifestyle changes that restore satisfaction.

All of us have a strong tendency to deny or minimize what is really happening. And after we do learn about our reality and acknowledge the truth, then we have to face our losses. We have to go through the inner process of grieving. It was as difficult for me as it is for anyone else, but I knew exactly what I had to do. "It's not terminal," is what the doctor said; I suppose he was trying to encourage me. But if I had had my preference, it would have been terminal so that it would come to a definite end. I prayed about it and about the purpose of my continued life. I do not know of any substitute for prayer in a situation like this. Today it is easier for me to look back at the steps I took in the first couple of years after FM set in. I'd say educating myself was first. I couldn't have done anything without knowing exactly what I was dealing with. Then I had to face the losses and go through the inevitable grief over them. I surrounded myself with supportive friends and family, but it was still a struggle emotionally to accept FM and the life alterations it brought. Next, I had to make changes and adjustments in every sphere of my life. But it is not all finished and over, as everyone here knows. It is an ongoing process. It takes a lot of my attention and effort every day to respond to the fluctuations in my condition and still remain positive and accepting toward life.

STEP TWO: TAKE RESPONSIBILITY FOR FINDING CARE AND LEARNING TO ADAPT

It's time to assume full responsibility for your care. First, you need the following comprehensive care:

- Regular sleep

- Good nutrition

- Stretching and limbering exercises

- Pool or other low-impact exercise

- Avoid overexertion

- Avoid weather extremes

- Rearrange household chores

- Restructure giving and receiving family roles

- Find your multidisciplinary medical team

- Physical therapy

- Adaptive training in all the domains of living

- Stress management training

- Personal counseling for blocks and traps

- Family or couples counseling for relationship struggles

Success in adjusting depends heavily on new skills learned at Step Two. Earnest work at this stage delivers a special bonus: you develop a degree of protection against setbacks because of stronger family alignment and the professionals you have recruited to help you meet the challenges of adapting. Your feelings of helplessness and vulnerability diminish. You feel much more in control of your life and how your future will work out.

- Task One: Assume responsibility for your complete care and take initiative for receiving adaptive training.

- Task Two: Set up caregiving and care-receiving roles at home.

- Task Three: Recruit complete professional care for your physical and emotional needs.

Joanne's No-Nonsense Approach to Education and Care

Along the same lines as her quick assessment and resolution of her condition, Joanne showed exemplary work at Step Two in taking an active role in educating herself about fibromyalgia and in setting up her comprehensive care.

I was ignorant—I had never heard of FM and neither had my family, friends, and associates at work; but we weren't ignorant for long. After receiving a diagnosis of FM, I looked up everything I could find on it. Many of my friends went online to find material. There were no support groups where I was located, and I personally knew of no one who would educate me about FM. I felt I needed to know everything about what was going on and proceeded to educate myself. I felt an urgency to learn as much as I could. Everything I learned I shared with my family and close friends. We needed that information in order for us to make adjustments. I can hardly conceive of dealing with FM without first being educated about it. You lose a lot of time if you are not informed. You can be pulled into useless treatments. You can get off on detours in medical care if you are indifferent about what is happening to you. I encountered doctors who didn't understand FM: one recommended surgery and another wanted to treat me with steroids. Neither of these treatments rang true with what I knew about FM, so I got another opinion. How thankful I am that I stayed on top of things and didn't go passively with the flow! It's entirely to my benefit to be informed about what I'm trying; no doctor has the time to explain everything. Things go much smoother if you do your part in educating yourself.

STEP THREE: REBUILD YOUR LIFE AND YOUR RELATIONSHIPS

Focus on building your relationships and your new life pattern in all six domains: self-worth; time and energy; family relationships; friends, relatives, and social circle; job or career.

Self-Worth

This is accomplished by introspection and intimate communication with your partner; it's where you regain your will to live a fulfilling life.

Joanne's Healthy Self-Esteem

Joanne was able to masterfully rebuild her life in part because of her healthy sense of self.

Fibromyalgia may seem like the end of the world for some people, people whose sense of identity is tied up in their outer world. But look inside! I'm still here. I may lose some external things, but my inner identity remains. Here is another way I look at it. Some of my medicines caused me to gain some weight. I sure didn't like that and spent quite a bit of money on diet plans, with no lasting results. But I need the medicine for my health and it's more important for me to take it than to worry about my physical appearance. My outer appearance has changed somewhat, but the inner person is the same.

Time and Energy

Correct time distortions by using planner books and other reminders. Learning how to manage your time allows you to gauge and pace your energy and accomplish your primary goals.

Joanne's Successful Time and Energy Planning

Joanne took important steps in managing her time and preserving her energy.

You start eating the right foods, whatever is best for your energy and health. You protect your sleep time so that you get regular, adequate sleep. You do low-impact exercises, or something similar, on a regular basis. You are careful about your energy expenditures. You learn to be flexible, since on any given day the symptoms may be more or less severe. You learn to accept assistance graciously. Never before did I have to be driven places in a car, but my arms and shoulders often hurt too much for me to drive. And I had to slow down my pace; there were many tears over that, but I did it. I just go at my own pace and avoid high-pressure situations the best that I can. But there is no end of interesting things to do. I love to study and communicate. And I'd say I'm a networker. I have a wide network of friends, many of whom have FM or a loved one with FM. We stay connected.

Family Relationships

Construct a new pattern of family living that makes allowance for the limitations of FM. Take on the roles that you are fully competent to do; these reconstituted roles do not strain you but do contribute to the family. The fourth domain is when you and your partner collaborate in structuring roles so that they are satisfying to both of you despite FM. A key to success is improved communication.

NICHOLAS'S STORY: SUPPORTING YOUR SPOUSE

Most families, when first hit with fibromyalgia, grope blindly and hope that this intruder will quickly depart. But who finally realizes that FM is here to stay and leads the family in building a new life pattern? Can the main support person embrace this role? Such was the case with Nicolas, who demonstrated exemplary emotional support for his wife.

My family's problem was not getting physical work done. We willingly pitched in and took care of all the chores. The problem was emotional distress. Although I kept affirming my love, my wife, Barbara, was not convinced. It seemed she needed proof. Here she was, frustrated, irritable, and at times distanced and withdrawn. She wondered how anyone could love her. The message I wanted to convey was that I treasured her even when sick. She didn't have to be perfect all the time; I loved her anyway. Finally, I convinced her by being patient and spending time with her. I took care to listen to her even when she was not feeling well. More than verbally affirming that I loved her, listening to her had greater impact. Appreciating her when she was not feeling well demonstrated my love despite FM. She accepted that and took comfort in it.

If you want to support your partner's self-worth and be close to him or her emotionally, you can't deride them for being ill. That destroys him or her. So you talk about the illness in a different way: "I hope we find things that help you feel better, but whether well or ill, my love for you is in no way diminished." If you berate your loved one for being ill, it will ruin your marriage. At your insistence, he or she might strive to do better, putting up a brave front and trying to bear pain and suffering without showing it, but the closeness in your marriage will be gone. For him or her to get through each day is a battle with FM. Your partner lives a strenuous life, and you wouldn't be alongside them in these struggles.

Friends, Relatives, and Social Circle

Learn tactics to deal with the reactions of friends and associates. You and your loved one are not helpless in the social setting. You can exert a degree of control in the manner in which you present yourselves. Each one of you will need to learn tactics to deal with the reactions of friends and associates.

JOANNE'S FRIENDSHIPS

Joanne's relationships with her friends, relatives, and her social circle took on new dimensions after she started rebuilding her life to make room for the changes due to fibromyalgia. She continued to maintain the success she had achieved in the way she handled friends and family who did not accept her condition and who put impractical expectations on her.

I have lost a number of friends but have made new ones. Some former friends refused to understand that I could no longer maintain the energy output that I used to. By making unrealistic demands on me, against my wishes, they were pulling me down. Of course, I explained to them about my situation, and some of them accepted it and wanted to continue their contact with me. Others did not. After a period of explaining, if I sensed that they were not going to come around, I just let them go.

Job or Career

Reconstruct your job or career—or avocation if you are not employed. Select a job that makes use of your highest-aptitude skills. Be creative in your thinking about how your current skills can be used in new and different ways. Don't take on too much.

JOANNE MAKES TOUGH CAREER DECISIONS

Joanne was able to use her skills as a counselor to work through her feelings about giving up her career in order to preserve her health.

I had difficulty walking, and for a while I couldn't drive because of my arms, but I was able to work one more year, thanks to my husband. He knew I was doing everything I could and helped me with the things I couldn't do. He saw, too, that FM fluctuates in its severity, with some days much better than others. So he helped me most on the worst days. But as you know, with a heavy schedule with constant pressure, FM tends to worsen. It became a losing battle and I had to give up my career. As a counselor, I felt as though I were being put to the test, to see if I could do the very things I had helped others do. I'm sure it did help, and I have to add that those close to me at work were also social workers and therapists. I was surrounded by supportive people. If I had not been, I would have wanted this kind of help for myself.

Step Four: Stabilize Fibromyalgia by Managing Stress and Crises

Protect what you have built to prevent setbacks. Develop these skills:

- Strategic planning for anticipated stress

- Relaxation techniques

- Assertiveness training

Setbacks are so common that they are expected occurrences. You and your family need to protect yourselves by learning from each setback and using what you learned to prevent them from happening. Sharpen your skills in detecting and managing stress.

9

WORKING AS A COUPLE TO ADAPT TO FIBROMYALGIA

◉

You and your partner need to adapt to fibromyalgia together. If you have no togetherness in this major life task, then the closeness between you quickly vanishes. In this chapter, we show you how to move through the adaptation process and face this illness together with your loved one. Throughout, examples from a couple who developed an exceptional collaboration confronting FM together—from her initial refusal to reveal her illness to the satisfying relationship they built despite FM—give you an inside look at working together with your partner.

COLLABORATIVE ADAPTATION

When faced with a life-altering chronic illness, there is a sequence of steps that you and your partner need to work through to adapt successfully. While you each go through your own individual adaptation process you will also need to learn how to make adjustments as a couple. These dual roles will be hard work, but you and your loved one can build a stronger relationship despite FM. There are several stages of reactions that you and your partner may cycle through as you address your new situation. You may stay stagnant in one stage for a while or change from day to day.

- A—A: Both you and your partner staunchly defy the reality of FM and make no adjustment for it.

- B—A: You try to make some adjustment while your spouse pushes the illness aside.

- A—B: Stances are reversed—your loved one may work on adjustment while you are in denial.

- B // B: Both you and your spouse perceive FM and its difficulties, but the strain leads to emotional distancing from each other.

- B—B: Caregiving and care-receiving roles are set up; solid communication is established.

- C—C: You and your partner together build a new constructive lifestyle.

The A, B, and C stages correspond roughly to the first three steps of the Four Steps to Adaptation. The following sections show in more detail the realities of some of these stages.

Working Through Denial
(A–A, B–A, A–B)

If you are like most couples, position A—A is the common first response after receiving a diagnosis of FM. You both refuse to believe that this illness is a reality in your lives. It is easier than trying to address the fact that one of you is ill and suffering from pain, severe fatigue, forgetfulness, clumsiness, insomnia, distressed emotions, and many other symptoms. Gradually, as the symptoms of FM intrude, your marriage may become tense. It will be more difficult to ignore what is going on. One of you may be more ready to embrace adjustments while the other is reluctant. You or your partner may become annoyed, disappointed, and angered because of losses of comfort and the disruption of your usual lifestyle. Your spouse may feel unsure about the marriage when he or she realizes that the symptoms of FM are not going to vanish and that life will not be the same.

In this initial denial, you and your partner may attempt to carry on as before, with you making superhuman efforts to sustain your prior activities, to the detriment of your health. You will find FM slowing down your lifestyle despite all your efforts and may then attempt to eradicate FM as though it were an attack of gallstones. At this point, you may embark on a frenzied search (see Chapter 3) to find anything that promises a cure and continue hunting until total eradication is achieved. To make sensible adjustments may be perceived by both of you as giving in and losing the battle. Nevertheless, both you and your spouse will eventually be compelled to deal with FM in some way—at first awkwardly and then more constructively.

RYAN AND ANNE'S INITIAL DENIAL

Ryan and Anne have been married eight years and are still going strong despite the fact that Anne has had fibromyalgia for over ten years. Ryan works as an airline pilot, and Anne is a flight attendant. Before meeting Ryan, Anne had been married to someone who did not attempt to understand FM. As a result, Anne did not reveal to Ryan that she had FM before they were married, and they both went through a lot of denial in the beginning of their marriage. Anne explains:

I had received a definite diagnosis of FM and went to medical doctors a number of times; I tried several medicines, but they did not help, so I stopped going to doctors. And I'm not one to moan about pain, so I put my foot down and just kept going with my life as usual. I had responsibilities. I had my job, my husband, my family, and my friends, and they came first. I tried to be cheerful, helpful, outgoing, and energetic despite how I felt. Usually, I could drive myself hard for two or three days. Then my body refused to go on. I couldn't work—the pain and fatigue were overwhelming. My brain also refused to work. It was a body-mind collapse, and I loathed the idea of being forced to stop and rest. But it was the only way to recover. It took several days of rest, then I could go again.

Ryan's response to changes in Anne's behavior:

I knew I loved Anne like I never loved anyone else. But this illness business was a puzzle, especially these collapses when she did not feel like doing anything. At work, she was 100 percent vivacious. If a person at work or a relative called and asked for her help, she managed to burst into energy, but it was very temporary. Soon she collapsed again. For me, it was a mystery—she had energy for everyone but me. I'd say, "Let's go horseback riding." She'd say, "I don't feel like it; it hurts too much." I still knew nothing about FM, and her behavior was a total mystery. She was a fireball of energy for everyone but me. The prospect of leaving her did come up, but I didn't say anything yet. I was desperate to find ways to make her feel better. So, I watched her carefully and noticed that her sleep was terrible—too much tossing and thrashing. No wonder she awoke tired and sore. My sleep was ruined just being next to her, and I figured her sleep was ruined, too. I inspected our bed. The surface was uneven and it had a sagging box spring. I replaced it right away. She seemed to sleep better, so I guess it helped, but her problems seemed to never end. The mystery seemed to deepen, and I watched for any clue I could find.

Sometimes when you become aggravated you say things you later wish you hadn't. I said to her, "I don't think I can do this." She knew fully what I meant. It crushed her. She was in tears for hours. Then she went to the other room and found a brochure for me to look at. The brochure had a diagram of a woman, eighteen tender points, and the name fibromyalgia. *We had gotten past a major hurdle. I now had a name and some information about her condition.*

DISTANCING AND BREATHING SPACE (B // B)

The two slashes in B // B represent a commonly encountered pause in you and your partner's interaction. Your interaction comes to a standstill as both of you ponder the difficulties you face. In evaluating your interaction, observe whether any of the following characteristic reactions apply to you.

• You and your partner feel overwhelmed, subdued, or weary with your problems, and neither of you wishes to discuss them or deal with them for a time. As a result, you both carry on in a mechanical way without any communication.

• Your roles and usual ways of performing tasks in your household have broken down and new ones are not in place yet; your relationship is at an impasse.

• You or your loved one feels emotionally distraught by the challenges of FM and difficulties within your relationship. Emotional eruptions can bring communication between the two of you to a halt for a time.

• You bitterly resent having to accept help; as a result, your spouse resents the impositions of giving help. You both seek some breathing space before forging ahead with your new roles.

The B // B phase may be used advantageously to let the emotional pitch of your relationship cool down before restarting. It provides a respite for you and your partner if you are continually confronting each other; it may also be an opportunity for you to realign yourselves to the new reality. What happens next is determined largely by the original reasons you married.

• Did you marry for external reasons, such as social enjoyment, shared recreational interests, sexual exchange, and increased income? If common interests are the only things forming the basis for your marriage and FM disrupts them, your marriage will likely be threatened. Even if you and your partner remain together in the same house, you may not be connected by the same things that originally brought you together. This impasse may be your signal to reexamine the basis for your marriage and to find a new purpose for being together.

• Did you get married to enact male-female roles in a family setting or to have children? In this case, your family roles need to be adjusted. With FM, you can still carry on as a husband or wife and father or mother, but some of your tasks and responsibilities need to be changed. Roles can be readjusted so that you are physically able to carry them out without removing the essential features of those roles. In setting up adjusted roles, your loved one starts pitching in to help where he or she can and assumes a support position in tasks and responsibilities where he or she sees you have difficulty. As your caregiving and care-receiving roles mature, they take on new character and become the normal pattern of your marriage.

• Did you get married because you were deeply connected to the fundamental self and identity of each other? If so, FM has changed nothing of essence, and your marriage is not threatened. For you and your loved one, FM is an external situation to be dealt with like any other challenge.

RYAN AND ANNE'S BREAKTHROUGH

During their years of adjusting to FM, Ryan discovered a massage technique that was helpful for treating Anne. Besides the relief of muscle pain, Ryan's persistence and willingness to help was a key factor in their ability to adapt to life with FM together. Ryan says:

Over the years, Anne and I tried too many "cures" to count. If the medical doctors couldn't treat Anne's fibromyalgia, I was determined to find something that at least would help—magnets, special diets, knuckle rollers (wooden massage devices). We hoped desperately that our remedies would work, and it seemed like each new one did help, at least to a degree, for a time. But then it became obvious that things hadn't changed very much. So we cursed our supposed cure and moved on to the next attempt.

It was during this time that I started reaching over with my hand to feel Anne's muscles, especially around the neck and shoulders. I felt large areas hard as bone—at least I thought I was feeling bone. Please understand at the time I knew nothing about bones and anatomy. Later, I learned I was feeling tense muscles. With practice, I began to make out individual muscles; sometimes they were soft, and sometimes they seemed like twisted cable. I noticed that when her muscles were taut, without exception, she was having a bad day. As far as I was concerned, this was a breakthrough discovery. I did not have to depend on her to tell me anything about how she felt, I could tell her. I was ahead of the curve and knew that she had better rest and recuperate. Even if she wanted to buzz around, I knew what would happen if she did. But I was still desperate in my search for things that might help. I found a book that gave instructions on massage techniques. Using these techniques, I could release the tension in a muscle by massaging at a 30-degree angle across it. I learned that it was incorrect to massage a muscle on its long axis, or crosswise at 90 degrees. I studied the book from front to back and then told Anne, "I have found something that will revolutionize your life." Those were my exact words.

Anne adds:

I thought, "Yeah, sure, one more stab in the dark." Although I had given up, I was still amazed and touched by Ryan's persistence. If he thought it could help, the least I could do was give it a try. But this one worked. At least for me it did wonders. I later found out that massage is helpful for many FM sufferers, but not all. For me, after two hours of his massage technique, my pain was cut in half. I could do things. Maybe not everything, but he could get me out of a collapse using massage. And if the pain returned the next day, Ryan would get the pain out by repeating the massage. I've never felt so loved in my life. You can't imagine how moved I was that he would do that. Really, even if I hadn't responded so well to it, he made himself available and close to me even when I was feeling terrible. It meant everything.

ESTABLISHING CARE-GIVING AND CARE-RECEIVING ROLES (B—B)

The next crucial move toward working together through the Four Steps involves your spouse recognizing that you are living in distress and responding in a supportive manner. This supportiveness may be noticeable in simple things that then lead up to more crucial caregiving roles. First, he or she may stop objecting when you become tired quickly and retire to bed early or go on errands or outings alone if you do not feel up to it. Next, your partner must become proactive in offering help by voluntarily taking some of the obvious load off of you, such as laborious household chores, grocery shopping, or driving errands. Finally, your loved one's supportiveness needs to become an active interest in your illness and discovering what can practically and realistically be done. For example, he or she may accompany you to medical appointments or research FM and become your well-educated ally. Other examples of supportive roles include spotting changes needed in your living environment, such as more comfortable furniture and bedding; working out schedules that are more accommodating for you; and setting up a Jacuzzi or other equipment that will bring you some relief. Most importantly, your partner offers you his or her emotional support, seeking ways to comfort and encourage you.

Balancing Family Roles

When dealing with FM, roles in a relationship can become unbalanced in one of two directions, either toward excessive role activity or toward minimal activity. Taking on too much responsibility that it becomes exhausting is common and shows that the person with FM is not accepting or receiving support from loved ones. In some cases, it can turn into the supernormal reaction (see Chapter 3). In attempting to defy FM by performing at high speed despite your pain and fatigue, you may end up aggravating your condition. Your frustration and irritability rise to new heights, sacrificing your family's closeness. Therefore, it is necessary for you to permit others to perform some of the more strenuous roles and to allow yourself to receive assistance and support. Make sure, however, not to minimize your activity and maximize intervention on the part of your loved one, as you may become helplessly dependent while your spouse takes on too much and gets burned out (see Chapter 7).

The healthiest position is to receive assistance in the right amounts, which means receiving support without giving up all of your roles or undermining your self-worth. Your objective as a person with FM is to gracefully relinquish burdensome roles, while keeping helpful roles. You thereby continue to make a positive contribution and avoid any arrangement that puts you in the position of being a liability to your family.

Our current culture unfortunately does not encourage specialization in male-female roles. Women today are expected to maintain self-sufficiency in all areas, almost to the point of refusing assistance from others. Nevertheless, once you and your partner recognize the new circumstances, you need to communicate to comfortably adjust roles to fit your needs. One way to adjust is for the FM sufferer to adopt the role of providing your family with emotional nurturance. Whatever roles you choose, it is crucial that you continue to contribute to your family; few people can thrive emotionally without feeling they are in some way making a contribution. There is no pat answer for how to do this; you and your spouse must address the problem head-on and design your own family roles.

RYAN AND ANNE'S CAREGIVING AND CARE-RECEIVING ROLES

Ryan and Anne worked hard to establish roles that allowed Anne to make a contribution without overexerting herself. Ryan reports:

After I could directly determine Anne's muscle and pain status, I had no tendency at all to doubt her complaints. It was just the opposite. She would try to tell me she was doing super, but I could tell quite definitely when her condition was getting worse. On those occasions, I would be the one saying that she had better take care of herself and that we had better plan accordingly.

Anne says:

I've learned that honesty and love go together. Ryan loves and accepts me whether I'm weak or strong, energetic or wiped out, whatever I'm feeling. I can't blame him for being frustrated and confused if I try to hide something. Things are much improved, even if not perfect. I work fewer hours than I used to, and I rest up before trips. By going to the support group, I was able to find the name of a physician who had helped others. I made an appointment, and the physician prescribed some medicines I had not tried before, which were definitely helpful. We've also learned a lot on the topic of adapting to FM. And I've found a physical therapist who can do massage similar to Ryan's method, so Ryan doesn't have to do all the work, and I can get a massage if he is out of town.

Setting Up Communication

The second part of getting through stage B—B involves setting up a family environment where communication is a priority. The first task of communication is to redefine caregiving and care-receiving roles so that they are more satisfying to both you and your partner. Helpful questions for the caregiver include:

- How much are you able to do?

- How much can I do without making you feel useless?

- How do you feel about my taking on these responsibilities?

- How can I help in a way that shows respect for what you still can do well?

The care receiver may want to ask:

- Which tasks do you have time for and are willing to take on?

- Will certain tasks make you feel overwhelmed or resentful?

- How do you feel about taking on these responsibilities?

- Can we afford to hire help for certain times or chores?

FM is an emotionally charged issue that can typically suppress you and your partner's abilities to talk about your feelings and frustrations. If you don't acknowledge each other's feelings you may begin to wonder if your spouse really understands how much pain you are in or how powerless your partner feels about not being able to ease your pain. Suffering in silence is not fair and doesn't help either of you; consequently, it's absolutely necessary for you and your partner to learn how to communicate clearly in order to successfully adapt to your new life with FM. Most of us are not exposed to methods of effective communication as we are brought up, so you may not know where to start. The resources in this book offer some suggestions to open up conversation.

Couples therapy is another way to develop communication skills. A counselor can guide you through exercises so you can recognize when each of you is having a difficult time and offer practical suggestions on how to open each other up and offer support. You may learn how to ease the tensions when they begin so you will not need outside help to avoid major conflicts. With a counselor you and your spouse may explore cooperative problem-solving techniques and amicable resolution of differences that can help you work as a team to reconstruct your lifestyle. You may also learn how to reestablish your connection as well as how to comfort each other, perhaps to an extent that you did not have before FM came into your lives.

Despite the benefits of couples therapy, you or your partner may still resist seeking out the help of a counselor. You may find that you are embarrassed about needing help, or you may not understand what therapy is. Perhaps you fear that the therapist will take sides or that you'll be seen as crazy if you need counseling. In the long run, your willingness to work with a professional is a true reflection of emotional maturity.

The experience of couples therapy can be pleasant, and it is certainly productive. With the counselor's help, you quickly reach the B—B phase and are well on your way to C—C. Typically, the least reticent partner sees the therapist first for a few sessions, and then the other partner starts attending the sessions jointly. Other specific ways of finding and working with a therapist are found in Step Two (see Chapter 4).

Ryan and Anne's Communication

Ryan and Anne proved a model couple in their willingness to communicate openly to work through the many challenges of FM. Ryan notes:

Even if you don't do massage, you can teach yourself what a sore, tight muscle feels like. Counseling without question would have saved us years of struggle, but we didn't even know such a thing existed. A counselor with some understanding of FM would have helped immensely. Instead, we worked out a system so that we would not get irritated with each other. We kept a clear understanding that the final decision always rested on Anne. That worked fine. Even when she paid no attention to my suggestions, it didn't bother me. I let her know that I respected her and loved her anyway, no matter what her decision was.

Anne says:

I do the shopping myself if it involves lightweight items. The rest of it we do together, but it is seldom like a chore. Even going to the grocery store, we play, laugh, joke around, and have fun. Some people notice us and stop to talk, and maybe others think we're crazy, but we don't worry about it. Ryan is great. I've learned to wait and let him offer to help. For example, I'll say, "I'll be cleaning the house." Maybe he is tied up on the computer and can't help immediately, but he'll say, "I'll join you in twenty minutes." Then we begin having fun. Women can be too serious, too much in control of the household—"Get that blasted room cleaned up!" If they have FM, they're going to be even more serious and somber. Where is the fun? No one prohibits you from playing and having fun, even if you are an adult woman or if you have FM.

There are the day-to-day fluctuations that you can ride through. Even though they are unpredictable, your determination can make a difference, so that you don't let them ruin your morale. But those are different from the collapses and recoveries that I have described in myself. Yes, I overdid things, then collapsed, and recovered. These were predictable, and they are manageable. I manage them by saving up energy. For example, when I'm scheduled to work for several days, I rest up for several days in advance. I've learned to say "no" to a lot of things, just so I can lollygag and rest at home. That way, by the time the first day of work comes along, I'm at my peak and ready to go at it for a few days.

THE ADVANCED COUPLE (C–C)

How does a mature relationship operate? What is the communication like? What are the giving and receiving roles like? The following insights can give you perspectives on what your relationship might look like once you reach the advanced, C—C, stage.

• Intimate communication is an important feature of your relationship. The doors are open for you to share your life with your loved one. Whether heartache or happiness, your spouse listens to and appreciates your experiences as well as finds ways to validate your personal worth.

• You and your partner are allies, collaborating and planning together. You and your loved one do more than merely tolerate each other's views and negotiate mutually acceptable solutions. You often experience satisfaction in your teamwork in addition to the satisfaction of accomplishing a task. You also find strength and composure in dealing with the world that is not possible when working in isolation.

• Rote, mechanical roles give way to carefully designed roles. You receive help in those specific areas where you require the help, and the roles that you are still able to carry out are reserved for you alone. Roles that are recognized as yours are respected by your family. You and your partner make sure that you do have roles that make you valuable to the life of your family.

• Your loved one is given ungrudging freedom to do things that you cannot do. He or she no longer feels guilty for doing things that you cannot do, such as playing tennis or hiking in the mountains. By intimately sharing your experiences, both you and your partner feel yourselves participating in the other's life.

• Both partners work continually to make adjustments. You and your partner are aware of the constantly shifting needs within your marriage and your family, and you work to accommodate those needs.

Communication is key to making steady progress in refining your pattern of living. Collaborative adaptation involves constant communication with your partner and respecting the limitations imposed by FM by arranging your lives so that you can enjoy your relationship together.

After we help ourselves individually and learn how to collaborate with our partners we can then reach out and help others with FM. We discuss this further in Chapter 10.

10

BRINGING COMFORT TO OTHERS

◉

It's time to celebrate: the days of "crisis living" are over! (But, be careful not to overexert yourself.) You have accepted your new life as an FM person and have made it through the Four Steps of Adaptation. It's time to enjoy your satisfying new lifestyle, but your new goal is to maintain it forever. Don't be surprised that this is an ongoing learning process that requires continuous work. Expect challenges that try to interrupt your routine every day, and use your skills to address any problems before they get out of hand.

We call this the "growth and maturation period" because there is constant movement—you're always striving to go forward and at the same time are ready to prevent anything from interfering with your success. Once you have learned to control FM instead of letting it control you, life begins to take on a renewed sense of meaning and purpose. The end of this journey brings restored function and a better quality of living that is worth all the hard work.

Friends, family, and coworkers will notice a difference in your attitude and composure as well as the boost in self-confidence that comes with success. There is no way you can hide the fact that you are happier being in charge of life instead of being run over by it!

You can be a quiet advocate by providing moral support to a few or an active participant in your community. Without making any effort beyond maintenance, you have become a role model, a touchstone person, for others. As a *touchstone* person, you are able to find purpose, meaning, lightness, and love in the face of adversity. You have the skills to defuse unruly emotions, soften angry confrontations, and provide perspective and long-range views. Just living a better life will be an inspiration to others, but as a graduate of "the steps" and a living success story, you have the power to teach and influence others, who then can appreciate that they can do it, too.

When we started building this program ten years ago, there were three people having coffee and researching educational material. Within six months, these three had grown to over a hundred, and we were taping an interview for Channel 5 in Las Vegas, Nevada. From that small seed, came FMFSG, Fibromyalgia Friends Support Group—which now numbers in the thousands. Three people and three words, "Pass it on" started what has become our "Four-Step Plan for Managing FM and Leading a Fulfilling Life."

The answers came to us from constant contact with other fibromyalgia people, their friends, and family members. The process of adapting to FM involves you and every other person in your life. It is something that is difficult to take on or manage alone. The lucky ones among us have families and friends to help us and access to medical care, along with other FM people for support. It is easier to succeed when you know others with FM.

We have found that nothing helps you more than being involved in some way with another FM person or a support group. Why? Because you need a relationship with someone who truly understands your situation and no one, regardless of how much they love you, can really understand this illness unless they have it. Having at least one FM friend is essential to your own continued success. If you are a quiet person, we urge you to practice speaking out by reaching out to people in support groups on and off the Internet. This practice will only add to your skills as an advocate for yourself.

There is a difference between caring family members who have learned about fibromyalgia and your FM friend because the latter needs no explanations about anything. You absolutely deserve the comfort of being around someone who can just look into your eyes and know what you are feeling without a word being said.

As a successful adaptor, you will not have to seek out people who need your help because they will find you. Word gets around, and if you are doing well, others will come to find out how they can do it, too. Anyone who has mastered the Four Steps can become a magnet attracting others who desperately need your help. Each day, as you grow and mature in your new life pattern, you learn more to share and gain confidence in how to pass on this knowledge.

If you are the ambitious type, who likes to reach out to others, you are a special gem because not everyone has the same motivation to change. Books like *Living with Fibromyalgia* let people know that they are not alone, and the Internet has opened doors of anonymity and communication to FM sufferers who do not have families or people to talk to.

You can truly help others by being available in whatever setting you choose—in the work place, in your leisure, by phone or e-mail. Your presence at support group meetings, or anywhere else for that matter, and your willingness to meet and talk with others has the greatest impact. There are hundreds of thousands of people who want to make contact with anyone with information on fibromyalgia. It's an amazing gift to be available when others need help and encouragement.

There is no question that you will meet some people searching for help through word of mouth, but how do you help the most people in the least amount of time with minimum effort? Many really do enjoy the privacy and confidentiality of a support group setting because they can become totally involved for an hour or so and then go home to the regular world and forget about discussing fibromyalgia until they feel like it again. Talking and listening one day a month may be enough. For those of you who are shy, keep in mind that you can make friends more easily if you are part of a support group or social circle.

What is the best thing you can do for another FM person? Just listen. We need to be heard. Save advice until they ask you a specific question. A smile, your comforting presence, and attentive listening are what they need the most. "Just being there" means the world to someone who has never met a fibromyalgia patient—let alone, one who is doing well.

It is extremely helpful to allow them to use you for an SUVV—a safe, understanding, venting vehicle. In times of extreme stress, your FM friend may need a sounding board to bounce off built-up frustrations! One of the best things you can do for each other is to express worries and concerns in private. It is okay to take turns harmlessly releasing pent-up feelings that make sense to both of you but that would only confuse friends and family. Instead of complaining or blowing up at home, try saving the frustration to let out in a safe place where no damage is done. It is comforting to know that you can maintain composure through a stressful day, then call an FM friend later and discuss whatever almost got you down.

One of the great things about having friends with FM is that you can openly discuss how to deal with problems if you feel like it or you can just enjoy each other's company. It is usually nice to not overload others though. Be sure to touch base when you have good days as well as when you have bad days. Be aware of how you are coming across.

For many FM people it's easy to meet, connect with, and share helpful information with others who have fibromyalgia—especially after you have traveled through the adaptation process. Our support group members describe being able to spot a stranger who has FM just by the way someone gets out of a chair or bends down to pick up a package. A familiar sound or gesture may tip you off that you have stumbled upon someone with fibromyalgia before even being told about it. It is true that FM people do share similar characteristics that others would never notice, but intuition can tell you when this happens. The longer you deal with this illness, the more attuned you become to the sounds and feelings that go along with it—and the easier it is to be helpful to those in need of support who might not have the courage (or might not know how) to ask for it. So a great part of the joy of your new life can be passing on the lessons you have learned at every opportunity.

As a graduate of FM adaptive training, you are a walking resource for not only other FM patients, but also the world in general. Each day that you are functional and happy, you are giving back to those who taught you how to succeed. Chances are very good that your efforts to share, care, educate, and pass on these helpful life lessons will make their way back to someone who touched your life when you needed help. When you become involved in passing on life-changing and life-saving information on how to cope with fibromyalgia, reaching out naturally and sincerely has a way of going full circle. We wish you much success and happiness in rebuilding and maintaining a meaningful life.

APPENDIX A

Case Studies in Adapting to Fibromyalgia—Insights from Daniel T. Shiode, Ph.D.

Daniel T. Shiode, Ph.D., is a clinical psychologist who specializes in pain psychology. He works primarily with individuals and families as they adapt to painful medical illnesses, including fibromyalgia. Many of the clients he sees are referrals from physicians. While counseling helps patients control the pain and cope with the life ordeal of chronic illness, themes in therapy for FM sufferers are not automatically the same as those found in regular therapy. The following three case studies highlight some of the major struggles that FM sufferers and their families face: feelings of loss, difficulty dealing with family and friends, and the people-pleaser trait. Dr. Shiode offers insight and advice into these cases to help you get a handle on this illness.

CASE STUDY ONE: DEALING WITH DENIAL AND LOSS

Maxine, a contracting agent with a major firm, was recently diagnosed with fibromyalgia. Maxine is best described as a Type A personality, constantly on the go and traveling all over the United States in her promising career. After the diagnosis of FM, however, she had to take a leave of absence because she could hardly work. Over a period of months, it became increasingly apparent to her that she would not be able to continue at her previous pace. She reluctantly applied for disability benefits, hoping that her health would improve; a year later her symptoms remain about the same.

Dr. Shiode: "Maxine is facing substantial losses. As I listen to life stories such as this, in many instances the affected person hardly can believe how many major changes have occurred in a short time. We do not know if Maxine's family members have been accepting toward these changes, but we do know that people with FM are told reams of nonsense by well-meaning friends. My first task is to validate her condition and to find out what the illness is doing to her. The next focus in therapy is *grief work*, where the individual comes to emotional closure on the losses sustained. Maxine is a business executive who has lost much of her ability to work. Her job may have been the main pursuit in her life, which gave her satisfaction and prestige as she advanced in her career. She has also lost part of her Type A coping style—she is no longer able to use this kind of drive to get things done. These are major losses. Of course, her secret wish is that these losses are fiction. Her sorrow is great and very understandable. It is likely that Maxine will experience anger about it. We would not want to deprive Maxine of all hope of ever getting "cured", yet we would want her to understand the chronic nature of this illness so that she can manage it realistically.

"People with chronic illness like FM can also experience a crisis of faith—they can feel angry with God. A valuable discussion on this topic is found in Rabbi Harold Kushner's book *When Bad Things Happen to Good People*. Reading it can help, but everyone dealing with such losses has to feel the heartaches before resolving them. Tears are necessary, good, and a sign of strength, contrary to popular opinion. Resolution can come after the tears and anger are expressed."

CASE STUDY TWO:
HANDLING FAMILY AND FRIENDS

Jennifer has FM, is in her early thirties, and is married with children. She is vivacious even when in pain, so from appearances few suspect that she has FM. Her family thinks she is lying outright, that she is using illness as an excuse or put-off. Jennifer had always been active doing things with her family and friends, but she now finds it draining even when her friends come to visit. Her dream is to finish school and begin a career when her children are older. She is concerned about her marriage, since she does not feel sexually inclined, stating, "I'm not a fraction of the woman I used to be."

Dr. Shiode: "Jennifer has her family to consider, plus an active but diminishing social life. We would want to protect Jennifer's health by easing the social demands yet maintaining her social life. Her vivacity may be misrepresenting her health status, concealing the fact of her illness. We would also keep in mind that Jennifer's vivacity may be a source of strength for her. In therapy, we would explore ways of presenting her family with a more realistic picture. In this way, she could make changes to convince her family of her actual status and regain their respect.

"Her young children also need to know about the illness, but it needs to be told to them in concrete terms, according to their ability to understand: 'Mother hurts; here is where it hurts.' But they also need to know that their mother's affection for them has not decreased. They need to know that she will survive despite being ill. A child's perception can be quite literal, and illness in a parent can evoke fears about separation and loss, so they need reassurance on this score along with the facts of the illness. The exact type of activity that an FM mother does with her kids may change because of FM. She may not be able to go to Disneyland or to play Frisbee in the park. A mother might feel guilty about not being able to run around and play with her kids like she used to, but she can still take an active interest in them. There can still be moments of loving communication and tenderness—this is the part of the relationship that counts. An important thing for a mother to avoid is to become needy and dependent on her own children for affection. A mother's role is to provide affection for her children—not to switch roles so that the children become responsible for how their mother feels.

"Jennifer's husband cannot avoid feeling the impact of the losses. Likely, he is experiencing sadness that Jennifer is ill and lethargic. He has lost a portion of the woman he married. It would be natural and necessary for him to grieve. The process of grief is similar for him as it is for Jennifer. So he, too, realigns his life so that it fits the new reality. FM has created a multitude of changes including changes in sexual relations. Here is the common error: to try to hold on to everything as it had been in the past and to avoid any discussion of change. Unfortunately, this tack does not work. To move forward, Jennifer and her husband will need to actively explore new ways to retain their emotional and sexual closeness.

"Once an FM person is in counseling, a spouse might come after learning that the therapist is keen on learning his side of things. The therapist can also open the door by sincere interest on his input regarding the difficulties that they share. Jennifer has individual concerns, plus she has ones affecting both partners together. So I'd want to involve Jennifer's husband to be able to deal with the difficulties that affect them as a couple. Commonly there are communication problems that plague the marriage that we would need to work with. Sometimes it is better to start with an individual session for the spouse. This is especially so when he has his own particular concerns and feelings about her illness and how it has affected their lives. Dealing with individual problems early makes later sessions with the two of them more productive. However, if the partnership is robust from the start, we can move right to couples therapy.

"Jennifer may be brooding on things she can no longer do. But there is the positive side of this question: What can she still do well? What are her strong suits, and which of these are intact and possible for her to do? Jennifer may not have the same career options that she envisioned, but there can be plenty of options open. If Jennifer is vivacious, she can likely find other ways to utilize this skill. I think we can devise ways for her to have a rewarding life. We would define 'rewarding life' in terms achievable for Jennifer. There might be less travel and less physical exertion, but she still has plenty going for her. She has her mind, her heart, and her vivacity. She has avenues in which she can be productive, including with her family. We would have to set aside stereotyped notions and the pressures that society exerts concerning 'success.' It is Jennifer's call; she decides what success means to her.

"Adapting to FM is never successful until a person fully acknowledges the reality of the illness. Life itself is the best instructor here, and we would ponder its lessons. She would need to release her self-image of the past and incorporate an image of herself as someone who has FM. There is no need for it to be a negative self-image; she can incorporate positive features, such as her ingenuity in making her life successful despite illness."

CASE STUDY THREE: OVERCOMING THE PEOPLE-PLEASER TRAIT

Misty, her husband, Eric, and their two children moved to a rapidly growing city for business reasons. Misty's fibromyalgia at the time of the move was not severe enough to interfere with her work. Her husband was a broker for a chain of dealerships, and he soon discovered that Misty performed well as an on-site sales trainer for the new dealerships as they opened. The family moved into a roomy house and hired a housekeeper. Misty began working at a relentless pace despite her symptoms of FM, which steadily worsened over the next several years. Socially, she had a full schedule, mostly with salespeople. Her clients clamored for her attention, and at home, her phone rang with hardly a pause between calls. Not only clients, but also family members, relatives, and friends called to discuss personal matters. Although her time was already at a premium, she was unable to say "no" or to set practical limits. She placed others' needs ahead of her own, a practice that overextended her physically and emotionally.

Eric supervised her closely. Viewing Misty as a valuable asset, he kept vigil on her, asking her to carry a pager and cell phone, and to report in to him throughout the workday. It was an unequal relationship as he declined to report his activities, expenditures, or schedules to her. He worked the top end of the business and made use of Misty's services as an assistant. Nevertheless, she was pleased about the arrangement. Misty readily admitted to feeling hurt whenever she failed to please someone. The diagnosis of FM had already been made, but she did not have time to go for regular care. She represented herself as a healthy person and went on at full speed, attempting to disregard her pain and fatigue. But periodically she collapsed, not for a day or two, but for weeks of total shutdown. She confined herself in her own house where she slept all morning, took long baths, and spent the day in a robe and slippers. She rarely ventured out. By unplugging her telephone, she disconnected from her flock. She canceled her seminars with excuses like having a migraine or the flu. The respite was refreshing at first, but soon she felt torn apart with conflicting emotions. She phoned her flock, reentered her former social circle, and was soon as involved again as though nothing had interrupted her.

After several years at this strenuous pace, Misty could not continue working any more. Her performance had dropped to the point that she and her husband decided to sell out and retire. Retirement brought Misty no respite from the telephone. When not on the phone, she catered to Eric. The irregularities in her living pattern remained largely unchanged. She followed no sleep schedule and did not exercise. She also did not have regular medical care except that now she saw a specialist for pain medication.

Dr. Shiode: "For Misty, the people-pleaser trait is obvious in listening to her description of herself. Hardly any part of her life is not affected by this trait. The compulsion throws all her relationships out of balance and creates difficulties in almost all areas of living. Look at how Misty is being rewarded by others for doing things that are detrimental to her. Look at how she overexpends her energy on others and hurls herself into collapses. As you well know, you don't do those things with FM! Misty is too focused on pleasing others and is sacrificing too much of herself in the process.

"It would hardly be possible to get around the people-pleaser trait in therapy. We could work on adapting to FM and related matters, but the trait would constantly interfere in our efforts. For the marriage, we want to understand how it is functioning. In this instance, we see that Eric's control over Misty is excessive. But Misty favors the arrangement. She is exceedingly good-natured about it, and she gets gratification by obliging him. But really, is the marriage so unequal in power? This would bear checking out. Is she in fact a subordinate? I don't think so, at least not completely. Since she is the deal clincher, she is holding power that she chooses not to exercise. She wants to avoid the clash or confrontation that would occur if she insisted on having equal say-so. We sense that she is approving, even encouraging, toward the lopsided relationship. Eric appears to have an unruly side, but she just smoothes out the ruffles. Smoothing ruffles is her specialty, an extraordinary talent that she uses at meetings in the new offices. She wouldn't give this up, since she derives satisfaction from doing it.

"Misty's social life is fine, except that she cannot curtail it when it goes into overtime, so it runs her ragged. Misty's health would improve if she put a limit on her contact with friends and clients. She would benefit by restricting time spent on the phone. Stresses would be decreased if she put limits on her speaking engagements and made use of a planner. I also recommend that everyone have time set aside just for relaxing. I would teach her relaxation skills. At the end of sessions, I often offer relaxation training to help my clients go into deep restful states. She could practice doing this at home, but there would be a hitch in this plan—her compulsion to please would deprive her of time for relaxation. In other words, her schedule would not budge, so there would be no time for a more relaxed lifestyle.

"Looking at her job aptitudes, her current work fits her perfectly. Work in human resources is exactly the field where she belongs. There would be no need to make changes in the kind of work she is doing. Rather, her big hurdle is to make changes in the intensity of the work she does. She would need to reduce her hours at work and turn off the phone when she gets home. She needs moderation; try as she might, however, she is not likely to succeed since her compulsion stands in the way. With this approach, Misty would look at all these indiscretions in detail and realize what they are costing her. Hopefully she would see how much better it is to gauge and pace.

"In reality, you can't just rip this trait away from her. It would never work in a client with such a deeply planted compulsion because by pleasing people, Misty nurtures her wounded sense of self-worth. It costs her, but the payoff is considerable. If treatment deprives her of these satisfactions, then pretty soon she will slip back into her previous modus operandi. She will find ways to circumvent any form of change. She has been driven by the trait to amass these props to her self-worth. Maybe she has succeeded with props, but she has not succeeded in freeing herself from the compulsion. Her innate self-worth remains as before, injured and hiding beneath the surface. Her life is relentlessly driven by it.

"To proceed, we would need to deal directly with the wounds and blows that made Misty a compulsive people pleaser. We would need to heal the wounds that set off the people-pleaser trait in the first place and identify and examine the events that smeared Misty's self-worth. Now, you cannot pretend that this trait materialized magically out of the blue or that it was derived solely from social norms. Pleasing people with this intensity was something that was learned; it was set off by definite events in the past. So the task in therapy for Misty is to work through these inciting events. We would look at how they led up to her compulsions and then show her she has a choice. That would constitute a first step.

"With the people-pleaser trait, dealing with the past—the roots—is essential. We use the term *roots* to refer to the source of these compulsions that are buried in the past. If you pull a weed but don't get the roots, the weed comes back. In actual practice, I do not find it difficult to move from present to past or to connect past with the present. The past comes up naturally when we are reflecting deeply on the present. Did Misty have to please an obsessive mother or father? Were her parents perfectionists who demanded that she be perfect, too? And if she did not meet their expectations, how did they treat her? Were they callous or angry parents who were constantly demeaning her? Were there events of abuse or molestation? In all of these examples, the sense of self-worth is degraded. If parents are doing this, they can undermine the child's sense of self, not nurturing it, which should be their foremost responsibility. In Misty's case, she did not marry into a better relationship. Eric recognized Misty's people-pleaser abilities and treated her as an asset. He did not value her for her innate worth or for the precious person she is. The upshot is that Misty's present life duplicates the relationships she had in her childhood, the unhealthy kinds we talked about earlier. She remains driven to please others so that she can have a sense of approval.

"What stance does the therapist now take? Here is one of the key points in this type of therapy. For Misty to make progress, she needs someone who fully accepts her despite her past or current relationships. This is what the therapist does. The therapist accepts Misty as a person in her own right and gives her the respect that goes with it. At first, Misty may have trouble perceiving the therapist as someone she trusts. Trust takes time to develop in any relationship. If we are successful, after a number of sessions she will begin sensing the integrity in the relationship. Finally, having had a relationship in therapy in which she was treated as an equal and with respect, she will relate to others in a similar way.

"With Eric, what he needs and what he is willing to do could be quite different. What he has come to expect, even count on, from Misty will be thrown into question. Eric has been taking advantage of Misty's compulsion to keep things smooth. Now he will be forced to take more responsibility and be asked to change his ways. If Eric wants to grow and mature along with Misty, he would benefit from therapy. But if he wants no part of it, he may find it increasingly difficult to connect with Misty anymore.

"The choices, then, fall squarely on both Misty and Eric. If Misty does her work in therapy, she will be choosing new modes of relating. If Eric has a change of heart and also wants a better relationship, he can choose therapy and get help. Changes will also start occurring with Misty's FM. Once the people-pleaser trait is out of the way, she will give FM the care and attention it deserves."

APPENDIX B

Finding Suitable Employment—Insights from David Guyette, M.S.

Does fibromyalgia wreak havoc on your job or career? Or is it the other way around—your job wreaks havoc on your FM? In our culture, the work ethic usually wins over the health ethic, driving us all to the edge of endurance. From our support groups, we have found that most employed FM people are sacrificing their quality of life because of excessive job demands. We also found that many unemployed FM people would be willing to work if they could find a compatible job. While we do not advocate that everyone needs a job, we dismiss the idea that FM people are miserable victims unable to do anything except drop out of life. Even if you are not part of the labor force, you can contribute in other ways. You can be involved in interest groups or advocacy groups, or you can do volunteer work in addition to your active participation in the home. Many people with FM are able to work part-time jobs, less-demanding jobs, or seasonal jobs. And if the job is the right fit, some can work full-time with no harm to their health.

With all these possibilities, you need to have a systematic approach to finding a satisfying job that is not damaging to your health. Vocational counselor David Guyette, M.S., shares his strategies and methods for defining your career goals and for pursuing job leads until you have the one you want. In addition to his extensive experience with helping chronically ill people, David also has experience with FM as it affects one of his close family members.

THE SYSTEMATIC APPROACH TO YOUR JOB SEARCH

If you are an FM person looking for work, your goal is usually to find a decent job that does not require strenuous work or high-level energy output. To proceed with

SOCIAL SERVICE DISABILITY

The Social Security (SS) Disability Act was never intended to provide permanent disability, much less retirement. The intent was to grant benefits to the disabled person only until he or she could recuperate and get back to work. Proposals were submitted to lawmakers to limit disability benefits to five years. None of these proposals were actually passed. Nevertheless, most disability examiners view benefits as a temporary solution. The system has its flaws, and it leaves some disabled people in limbo, insecure about receiving future disability checks. However, few people know that the law actually allows you to try out jobs and earn some money for a year or two without losing benefits. The usual response you get to your first application for disability is rejection. However, the SS Disability Act is complex. You rarely get a disability rating the first try. The first rejection leads to the next step, an appeal for which you might need legal assistance.

If you want permanent disability, the SS Disability Act is a tough route to go, although there are those who manage to get it. The system works better for temporary disability. If you have recovered enough so that you can work if the environment is right, you can get help from your state's employment office. If you cannot do your previous type of work but can do other types of work, you can work with a vocational rehabilitation counselor at your state's employment office.

this goal, it is vital that you take an honest assessment of yourself. Do you honestly desire to find a satisfying job, or do you just want disability? Also, without kidding yourself, figure out what you precisely can and cannot do. What work limitations will you be entering into this equation? Once you have all this information up front, you can zero in on a good job match. In some instances, you may be disabled for every type of work; you have little choice but to apply for disability benefits. However, just because you have an illness does not automatically consign you to total disability. Whatever your status of FM may be, you should aim for a good match of working conditions.

Explore All of Your Opportunities

The first step to finding a good match of working conditions is to tour all of your available job opportunities. You can begin by looking through the classified ads. Then you can search through the following occupational handbooks.

- *Occupational Outlook Handbook* by the U.S. Department of Labor. This book provides information on jobs held by 90 percent of the U.S. workforce and is available at public libraries in the reference section.

- *Encyclopedia of Careers and Vocational Guidance*, Twelfth Edition, edited by Andrew Morkes. This four-volume text is also available in the reference section of your public library.

- *Job Search Handbook for People with Disabilities* by Daniel J. Ryan. This book provides step-by-step instructions on selecting a career or job, writing your résumé, conducting a search, interviewing for jobs, making accommodations for disabilities, normalizing disabilities to your coworkers, and keeping your job.

Almost anyone can find at least a few appealing listings for jobs by exploring these resources. You may be relieved to discover that you can still work and earn money and become more determined to do just that. By this one exercise, you will gain incentive to work and pick up ideas on appealing types of work.

Take a Self-Administered Aptitude Test

The second way to find a good job match is to take a self-administered aptitude test. You can try any one of the following self-administered job aptitude tests.

- *Discover What You're Best At* by Linda Gale. Features the self-scoring National Career Aptitude System (NCAS), which matches you with one of forty-one career clusters.

- *Square Pegs and Round Holes: How to Match Personality to the Job* by Lee Elston.

- *Career, Aptitude and Selection Tests: Match Your IQ, Personality and Abilities to Your Ideal Career* by Jim Barrett. Other books in this series include titles on CV writing, job search, and interview skills.

- *Career Tests: 25 Revealing Self-Tests to Help You Find and Succeed at the Perfect Career* by Louis Janda.

- *Test Your Own Job Aptitude* by James Barrett and Geoff Williams. This book helps you match your personality to a career choice.

You can also go online to the Vocational Research Institute (vri.org). This organization sells software for self-scored aptitude and career preference tests. The VRI website includes an evaluation system for individuals with special needs called "WorkPlace Mentor."

By taking one or more of these tests, you may discover aptitudes you never knew you had. Once you know your talents, you can narrow your search to jobs that call for these strengths. In addition, working at a job for which you have aptitude brings greater job satisfaction, and thus your job performance is likely to excel. When you excel at your work, you reduce work stress and drudgery. Despite all these benefits, however, very few people have analyzed their aptitudes, and rarely do schools provide any aptitude testing. Because it is a very worthwhile process, you should proceed immediately to test yourself.

Define Your Exclusion Criteria

Defining your exclusion criteria refers to the basis by which you exclude jobs from consideration. You will be able to quickly eliminate some jobs as possibilities because of these criteria. What are the automatic exclusion criteria when you have fibromyalgia? You may decide that outdoor work gets an immediate thumbs down. The same goes for heavy exertion, although some FM people say that they need to be mobile and are unable to sit motionless at workstations for long hours. Finally, you should almost always exclude high-intensity and high-stress jobs. While some people love stimulation and thrive on competition, with FM you should not even consider high-intensity jobs.

Be Realistic About Employers

In the real world, only rare companies have flexible job expectations. William Lareau, in his book *The Where I Am Now? Where I Am Going? Career Manual*, states that you are not likely to find a workplace that shows special consideration for individual employees. Most companies make glowing promises about how they pamper employees, but don't be fooled by this window dressing or listen to the fictions that companies tout as their official policies—that's not how they really deal with you. As an individual you may be unique, but to demand unique treatment will bring you nothing but trouble. Instead, you must learn the social skills to get along in the typical workplace.

REFINE YOUR JOB SEARCH

Once you factor in the reality of your company's policy, you can examine job descriptions from the various resources mentioned earlier in the chapter to estimate each job's intensity—high, medium, low. Sort the low-intensity positions into one pile, and cross off all the high-intensity listings. For medium-intensity positions, you might look for creative ways to decrease the intensity. For example, suppose you happen to discover a job of medium intensity that pays high wages. Would the employer consider making it a part-time position? By reducing the hours, you may be able to decrease the stress load.

Part-Time Employment

Part-time employment is underrated and should receive special attention by anyone with chronic illness. There are innumerable opportunities; for some types of work, the majority of openings are for part-time positions. For example, retail sales is mostly part-time work and can be a practical way to go. You could also investigate becoming a runner for an attorney or realty company, a pet sitter, a tutor, or a clerk in customer service. As fibromyalgia fluctuates in severity, seasonal jobs such as wrapping gifts, making hospitality baskets during busy times, assisting florists, or doing flower deliveries, may also be a possibility. While there are many types of jobs that fall in this category, you will need to be persistent to land some of them. If you apply for seasonal work at a retail store, for example, you may have to check back with them frequently. For busy-season retail work, start looking before Halloween. Another area for FM people to explore is security jobs, which often have a nice combination of low-intensity and part-time work. Contrary to the usual impressions, you may be able to sit down the greater part of your work hours.

Workplace Accommodation for the Chronically Ill

The Americans with Disabilities Act (ADA) was passed by Congress in 1990. It mandates that an employer with fifteen or more employees must make "reasonable accommodations" for disabled people. According to the ADA, you cannot be fired for having a disability as long as you can do your job, and you can have accommodation as long as it is "reasonable." The term *reasonable* is vague, and requests for accommodation are not always granted.

When considering work accommodation, you must first consider the matter of disclosure. Does your supervisor know about your disability? If not, do you want to disclose it? Many disabled people feel their health status is private information. However, if your illness keeps you out sick or otherwise draws attention to your status, you may have no choice but to tell your supervisor.

If you are willing to disclose your illness, you can often get accommodation if your requests are not excessive. If you are on good terms with your supervisor, a request for a minor thing such as a different chair poses no problems. In more formal settings, your supervisor may send your request to the human resources department. Thus, you should formulate your requests carefully. If you have a whole page of items for which you request accommodation, the human resources department may rule that you are incapable of working altogether. You are far more likely to get accommodation if you trim your requests to a bare minimum.

You cannot be too careful in seeking accommodation for FM. A vocational counselor can help you with this, or a friend outside your company who is in a supervisory position can talk with you over the advisability of these requests. Be sure to think about what will happen if the request is refused. Will you quit because you cannot do your job unless the request is granted? Are you willing to confront your employer over the matter? If your employer threatens your job, would you file a complaint under the ADA or take legal action? If not carefully handled, a simple request could escalate into a showdown. You may decide to resign rather than to subject yourself to stress of this magnitude.

Temporary Work

Temporary agencies, which send their employees out on temporary assignments, look for people with skills in a multitude of career areas. If they offer you an assignment, you can accept it or pass—a nice arrangement if you prefer to work episodically.

Working from Home

There are a variety of ways to work from your home. Teaching such classes as writing workshops or cooking classes requires talent in a specific area; it also requires a referral base or some kind of marketing. For example, music instructors, such as piano and voice teachers, can often get referrals from music stores or perhaps from churches. If you are very talented, this type of work can pay well. However, agencies that send office work to your home, such as addressing envelopes, can be highly demanding. They often have short deadlines, and the work may come in such hefty batches that it would stress almost anyone. An exception would be jobs for which you can use your computer, such as preparing résumés. You can find these types of jobs by doing an online search for "telecommuting jobs."

COMPLETE YOUR JOB SEARCH

The final steps that land you a well-matched job are to write résumés, fill out applications, and persist. In addition to the aforementioned *Job Search Handbook for People with Disabilities*, there are several places that you can get started in finding jobs that match your criteria.

- Job listings in the classified ads

- The *Yellow Pages* in the "employment" section

- Employment agencies, including your state's employment office

- Word of mouth through your friends, acquaintances, neighbors, relatives, and former associates

- Online with a computer, either at home or at your public library

- Online at various websites, such as America's Job Bank (www.ajb.dni.us), Career Builder (careerbuilder.com), CareerPaths (careerpathsonline.com), Hotjobs (hotjobs.com), and Monster (monster.com)

Remember that a job search is not idle. You cannot just pass time waiting for replies to your applications. You must be constantly working your leads. And the more people who are helping you, the better. Interestingly, statistics show that word of mouth is a more successful route to finding a job than any other. You must commit some time every day to working some angle of the search. Keep this up until you are ready to enter the workplace. Your search can take a week, six weeks, or occasionally six months. But if you know what you are looking for and persist in searching for it, you will likely find it.

Your job search can be done at home, telephoning people, writing letters, or working online. Part of the work may also be in-person contacts. For example, just because you have sent out job applications does not prohibit you from talking to an employment agent. If an agent can open a door in a direction you want, you pursue this too. The key is to know precisely what you want. Job-finding agencies charge a commission with the exception of state employment offices. Don't view the state employment office as a last resort, as most of them provide services to any citizen of the state, including those who are not receiving unemployment.

As discouragement and slow motion can be major problems right from the beginning, you may want to seek the help of a vocational counselor. A vocational counselor will work with you in getting a good match of working conditions and help see to it that your job search is constantly carrying you toward your goal. In addition, mental health professionals can help, as they can step right in as soon as you state your intention of doing a job search.

Summary

To find the right job that accommodates your fibromyalgia, you must apply a rigorous approach to your search. You must do the following tasks.

- Step One: Scan the opportunities available. Collect appealing ideas for jobs. Look in places with job listings, such as classified ads and online resources.

- Step Two: Identify your aptitudes. Take the NCAS or another self-administered aptitude test. Focus your search in areas where you have aptitude.

- Step Three: List your exclusion criteria. Know your limitations and eliminate jobs that overstep your capacity. You will probably want a low-intensity job, so include this in the selection process. Consider part-time or intermittent work to decrease your stress.

• Step Four: Start a job search when you have a good idea of what you are looking for. Submit applications and résumés and pursue your leads. Be persistent. Do at least some work every day on some angle of your job search.

Finally, from beginning to end, the assistance of a vocational counselor is invaluable for keeping you on track. If you cannot find one, a family counselor or psychologist may help you in these efforts.

RESOURCES

The Arthritis Foundation. *The Arthritis Foundation's Guide to Good Living with Fibromyalgia.* Atlanta, GA: The Arthritis Foundation, 2001.

Bennett, Robert M., ed. *The Clinical Neurobiology of Fibromyalgia and Myofascial Pain.* New York: Haworth Press, 2002.

Braunwald, Eugene, Anthony C. Fauci, Dennis L. Kasper, et al., eds. *Harrison's Principles of Internal Medicine.* 15th ed. New York: McGraw-Hill, 2001.

Charmaz, Kathy. *Good Days, Bad Days: The Self in Chronic Illness and Time.* Camden, NJ: Rutgers University Press, 1991.

Chino, Allan, and Corinne Davis. *Validate Your Pain.* Sanford, FL: InSync Communications, 2000.

Goldstein, Jay A. *Betrayal by the Brain: The Neurologic Basis of Chronic Fatigue Syndrome, Fibromyalgia Syndrome, and Related Neural Network Disorders.* New York: Haworth Press, 1996.

Goldstein, Jay A. *Tuning the Brain.* New York: Haworth Press, 2004.

Kubler-Ross, Elisabeth. *On Death and Dying.* New York: Scribner Classics, 1969.

Kushner, Harold D. *When Bad Things Happen to Good People.* 1981. New York: Random House, 2004.

Morgenstern, Julie. *Time Management from the Inside Out.* New York: Henry Holt, 2000.

Norem, J. K. *The Positive Power of Negative Thinking.* Cambridge, MA: Basic Books, 2001.

Royer, Ariela. *Life with Chronic Illness: Social and Psychological Dimensions.* Westport, CT: Greenwood Publishing Group, 1998.

Wallace, Daniel J., and Janice Brock Wallace. *Fibromyalgia: An Essential Guide for Patients and Their Families.* Oxford, England: Oxford University Press, 2003.

Worden, J. William. *Grief Counseling and Grief Therapy.* 3rd ed. New York: Springer Publishing, 2002.

Wright, Peter W. D., and Pamela Darr Wright. *Wrightslaw: From Emotions to Advocacy: The Special Education Survival Guide.* Hartfield, VA: Harbor House Las Press, 2001.

CAREERS AND JOB SEARCH RESOURCES

Barrett, James, and Geoff Williams. *Test Your Own Job Aptitude: Exploring Your Career Potential.* Reissue ed. New York: Penguin Books, 1984.

Barrett, Jim. *Career, Aptitude and Selection Tests: Match Your IQ, Personality and Abilities to Your Ideal Career.* London, England: Kogan Page, 1982.

Elston, Lee. *Square Pegs and Round Holes: How to Match Personality to the Job.* First Step Enterprises, 1984.

Encyclopedia of Careers and Vocational Guidance. 12th ed. 4 vol. New York: Ferguson Publishing, 2002.

Gale, Linda. *Discover What You're Best At.* Rev. ed. New York: Simon & Schuster, 1982.

Janda, Louis. *Career Tests: 25 Revealing Self-Tests to Help You Find and Succeed at the Perfect Career.* Avon, MA: Adams Media, 1999.

Lareau, William. *The Where I Am Now? Where I Am Going? Career Manual.* Winchester, ON: Winchester Press, 1997.

Ryan, Daniel J. *Job Search Handbook for People with Disabilities.* Indianapolis: Jist Publishing, 2000.

U.S. Department of Labor. *Occupational Outlook Handbook.* 2004–2005 ed. Indianapolis: Jist Publishing, 2004.

EDUCATIONAL RESOURCES

The National Fibromyalgia Association
Lynn Matallana, President/Editor
2238 N. Glassell Street, Suite D
Orange, CA 92865

To receive *Fibromyalgia AWARE* magazine, call 714-921-0150, e-mail nfa@fm aware.org or visit FMAware.org.

Fibromyalgia Friends Support Group
Patti Wright, Christy Nobel, Mattie Mitchell-Smith
2245 N. Green Valley Parkway, Suite 215
Henderson, NV 89014

To receive the newsletter and adaptive training information, fax 702-897-2801, e-mail FMAngels3@cox.net or noblepeople@aol.com or visit FMAdapt.com.

American College of Rheumatology
1800 Century Place, Suite 250
Atlanta, GA 30345
Phone: 404-633-3777
Fax: 404-633-1870
rheumatology.org

American Academy of Pain Management
13947 Mono Way, Suite A
Sonora, CA 95370
Phone: 209-533-9744
Fax: 209-533-9750
aapainmanage.org

American Pain Society
4700 W. Lake Avenue
Glenview, IL 60025
Phone: 847-375-4715
Fax: 877-734-8758
ampainsoc.org

Arthritis Foundation
P.O. Box 7669
Atlanta, GA 30357
Phone: 800-283-7800
arthritis.org

National Fibromyalgia Partnership
P.O. Box 160
Linden, VA 22642
Phone: 866-725-4404
Fax: 866-666-2727
fmpartnership.org

American Fibromyalgia Syndrome Association, Inc.
6380 E. Tanque Verde, Suite D
Tucson, AZ 85715
Phone: 520-733-1570
Fax: 520-290-5550
afsafund.org

Focus on Fibromyalgia
3333 S. Wadsworth Blvd.
Suite D312
Lakewood, CO 80227
Phone: 303-986-3339
focusonfibromyalgia.com

American Association for Chronic Fatigue Syndrome (AACFS)
27 N. Wacker Drive, Suite 416
Chicago, IL 60606
Phone: 847-258-7248
Fax: 847-748-8288
aacfs.org

National Institutes of Health (NIH)
9000 Rockville Pike
Bethesda, MD 20892
Phone: 301-496-4000
nih.gov

Find a Doc
findadoc.com

Irritable Bowel Syndrome (IBS) Self-Help and Support Group
1440 Whalley Avenue, Suite 145
New Haven, CT 06515

IBS Self-Help Group—Canada + International
P.O. Box 94074
Toronto, ON M4N 3R1
Canada
ibsgroup.org

National Sleep Foundation
Phone: 202-347-3471
Fax: 202-347-3472
sleepfoundation.org

National Headache Foundation
Phone: 888-NHF-5552
headaches.org

Americans with Disabilities Act (ADA)
Phone: 800-514-0301
TTY: 800-514-0383
ada.gov or usdoj.gov/crt/ada/adahom1.htm

Job Accommodation Network
P.O. Box 6080
Morgantown, WV 26506
U.S. V/TTY: 800-526-7234
Worldwide V/TTY: 304-293-7186
janweb.icdi.wvu.edu

Social Security Administration
Office of Public Inquiries
Windsor Park Building
6401 Security Blvd.
Baltimore, MD 21235
Phone: 800-772-1213
TTY: 800-325-0778
ssa.gov/reach.htm

National Center for the Dissemination of Disability Research
Southwest Educational Development Laboratory
211 East Seventh Street, Suite 400
Austin, TX 78701
Phone: 800-266-1832 or 512-476-6861
Fax: 512-476-2286
ncddr.org/index.html

INDEX

Ultra Balm, 24
Ultram as pain medication, 21
Unemployment, 53
Unexplained weight gain or weight loss
  in fibromyalgia, 9
Un-refreshed and interrupted sleep in
  fibromyalgia, 4–5
Urinary frequency in fibromyalgia, 7

Valerian root to treat insomnia, 27
Validate Your Pain (Chino & Davis), 32
Vertigo, 8
Veterans Administration, 53
Victimhood, sense of, 118
Vocational counselor, 162
Vocational Research Institute, 160

Walking, 25
Wallace, Daniel J., 17
Wallace, Janice Brock, 17
Weight gain in fibromyalgia, 9

Weight loss in fibromyalgia, 9
When Bad Things Happen to Good People
  (Kushner), 150
*The Where I Am Now? Where I Am
  Going? Career Manual* (Lareau),
  160
Widespread pain in fibromyalgia, 2
Williams, Geoff, 160
Worden, William, 42
Workplace accommodation for
  chronically ill, 162
Wright, Pamela, 79
Wright, Peter, 79
Wrightslaw: From Emotions to Advocacy
  (Wright & Wright), 79

Zanaflex, 22
Zelnorm for irritable bowel syndrome
  (IBS), 7
0 to 10 pain-rating scale, 81
Zoloft for depression, 6

ABOUT THE AUTHORS

Dean Mondell, M.D., has been in private practice in Las Vegas, Nevada, for over twenty years where he specializes in compassionate care of chronic pain patients suffering from severe injuries, trauma, and fibromyalgia. He is board certified in Physical Medicine and Rehabilitation, received his medical degree from University of Maryland, and completed his Internship and Residency at Sinai Hospital in Baltimore where he also served as Chief Resident. He has published several professional articles, is involved in hospice care and patient advocacy, and is a well-known motivational speaker for ill patients and their loved ones. Dr. Mondell is a member of the American Academy of Physical Medicine and Rehabilitation, the American Academy of Pain Management, and the American Congress of Rehabilitation Medicine. He serves on the Advisory Board for the Fibromyalgia Society of Las Vegas and is the medical advisor to the Fibromyalgia Friends Support Group, which serves over 1,500 patients.

Patti Wright is the founder and leader of the nonprofit educational organization Fibromyalgia Friends Support Group, which was established in 1996. Her organization's monthly newsletter, for which she has written hundreds of articles, has a circulation of 1,500 readers in 36 states, and she also writes regularly for *AWARE* magazine (National Fibromyalgia Awareness Magazine). She's a member of several national organizations, including the National Fibromyalgia Association (NFA), the Support Connection of the NFA (she is one of eight board members who serve over 1,200 support groups across the country), the National Fibromaylagia Partnership, and the American Academy of Pain Management.